Deconstructing Management Maxims, Volume II

Deconstructing Management Maxims, Volume II

A Critical Examination of Conventional Business Wisdom

Kevin Wayne

BEP BUSINESS EXPERT PRESS

Deconstructing Management Maxims, Volume II: A Critical Examination of Conventional Business Wisdom
Copyright © Business Expert Press, LLC, 2017.

First published in 2017 by
Business Expert Press, LLC
222 East 46th Street, New York, NY 10017
www.businessexpertpress.com

ISBN-13: 978-1-63157-791-8 (paperback)
ISBN-13: 978-1-63157-792-5 (e-book)

Business Expert Press Human Resource Management and Organizational Behavior Collection

Collection ISSN: 1946-5637 (print)
Collection ISSN: 1946-5645 (electronic)

Cover and interior design by S4Carlisle Publishing Services Private Ltd., Chennai, India

First edition: 2017

10 9 8 7 6 5 4 3 2 1

Printed in the United States of America

Dedication

To Alysandria and Leanne

Abstract

A contrarian challenge to the status quo, this book vigorously champions healthy skepticism in management theory and practice. Several common management maxims — often taken for granted as truisms — are examined and debunked with evidence-based arguments. The constant repetition of these flawed tropes perpetuates their mythological status and limits personal and organizational performance. Eleven management maxims are rebuked using empirical data, original scholarship, literature reviews, field observations, and thoughtful opinions from numerous experts. Examined in depth, the flawed maxims in Volume One include: Customer is King; People are Our Most Important Asset; Diversity Improves Performance; Competitive Advantage is Necessary to Compete; and A Business Plan is Required for Entrepreneurial Success. The maxims debunked in Volume Two include: Mission Statement is a Must; Learn a Second Language (other than English); Introverts Cannot Lead Effectively; Worrying is Counterproductive; Failure is Not an Option; and Consensus Decision Making is Optimal.

Far from a business as usual business book, *Deconstructing Management Maxims* has been researched with academic rigor yet written in an approachable style. Unafraid of taking on conventional business wisdom, it contains some controversial yet substantiated positions that will provoke critical thinking and debate. After all, sacred cows and long-believed tenets of management lore do not go away quietly. A clear message from this book is that you don't have to believe everything you read or hear— be it in the classroom or at work! It offers a refreshing break from the constant drumbeat of dronish corporate and academic clichés. This book is best appreciated by readers wanting to think critically about important management phenomena.

Keywords

business plan, competitive advantage, consensus decision making, contrarian, customer satisfaction, diversity, English language, failure, human resources, introvert, leadership, management, mission statement

Contents

Preface for Volume Two

Fallacies are not simply crazy ideas. They are usually both plausible and logical—but with something missing.
    —Thomas Sowell, *Economic Facts and Fallacies*

Wrong does not cease to be wrong because the majority share in it.
    —Leo Tolstoy, *A Confession*

In the first volume of *Deconstructing Management Maxims*, a thorough rationale for debunking several flawed maxims within the management lexicon is put forth for readers inclined to challenge the status quo. To recap, the five brazen and imperfect statements examined in Volume One include: *Customer is king*; *People are our most important asset*; *Diversity improves performance*; *Competitive advantage is necessary to compete*; and a *Business plan is required for entrepreneurial success*.

Volume Two of *Deconstructing Management Maxims* continues the work of disproving faulty and long-held tenets of conventional business wisdom. But before previewing the specific statements to be deconstructed in this volume, I feel it is appropriate to invoke the introductory sentence from Thomas Paine's 1776 pamphlet *Common Sense*, which proclaims the following:

> Perhaps the sentiments contained in the following pages, are not *yet* sufficiently fashionable to procure them general favor; a long habit of not thinking a thing *wrong*, gives it a superficial appearance of being *right*, and raises at first a formidable outcry in defence of custom. But the tumult soon subsides. Time makes more converts than reason.[1]

I refer to Thomas Paine's challenge, at the risk of sounding unoriginal and pretentious, to communicate the often contrarian nature of *my following pages*. Whether it was Paine's affront to accepted dogma two-and-one-half centuries ago or Aristotle's praise for maxims as an argumentative weapon over 2,000 years prior, it appears little as changed. Conventional wisdom continues to permeate culture with the brute force of its safety and acceptability. It is in the spirit of uncovering the truth in management theory and practice that I put forth the arguments and analysis included here in Volume Two of *Deconstructing Management Maxims*.

Six additional maxims are scrutinized in Volume Two with the aid of empirical analysis, observation and thoughtful commentary. Chapter One starts us off with the much heralded maxim claiming that a *Mission statement is a must* for success in business. Although a common inclusion in management, new venture, and strategy textbooks, as well as a starting point for management consultants to begin invoicing their clients, I have uncovered evidence showing that a mission statement is not as indispensable as once thought. This research has unveiled a surprising number of blue chip firms that do not subscribe to the mission statement mantra. A review of the literature as well as my own data collection and analysis of the S&P 100 and Fortune 500 are provided. Additionally, there is a short quiz you can take to test your corporate mission knowledge.

A rather controversial topic gets the critical treatment for Chapter Two. For years, Americans have been bashed for not knowing their world geography and for speaking only English, especially when compared to Europeans. However, I contend that the cry for English speakers to learn a second language is not nearly the necessity it has been portrayed to be. While I am a committed globalist and believer in the richness of intercultural competency, I subscribe to the widely held position that English is the lingua franca for international business. I debunk the overgeneralized rhetoric insisting that native English speakers *Learn another language*. This chapter also examines the trend of companies in non-English speaking countries adopting English as their official business language.

Chapter Three deals with the common yet mistaken notion that *Introverts cannot lead effectively*. Our culture tends to gravitate toward the boisterous and charismatic. We seem destined to follow those with outward confidence, extraverted leaders with enthusiasm and ceaseless energy. In contrast, I'll provide examples of accomplished leaders that are more sedate and reserved, yet as impressive as their chest thumping counterparts.

The act of worrying has gotten a bad rap over the last several years. Chapter Four's misleading maxim of *Worrying is counterproductive* is an outgrowth of all that research telling us how bad stress is for our health. Marriott Hotels ran an ad campaign recently spouting, "When you're comfortable, you can do anything," highlighting the comfy confines of their hotels. However, I'll provide several examples where sweating the details and staying up late pondering *what if* scenarios can yield tremendous benefits. A strong dose of healthy paranoia can be great for business.

The pop sensation maxim *Failure is not an option* (Chapter Five) is one that warrants particularly thoughtful criticism. While not a desired result, failure happens. If failure is feared too much or rarely seen in you, your team or your organization, then you are not pushing hard enough for growth and results. This chapter includes numerous examples extolling the benefits of normalizing failure.

Organizations often praise participatory and democratic management systems. The maxim for discussion in Chapter Six, *Consensus decision making is optimal,* has gained momentum from the movement of progressive team management techniques. However, consensus is often employed by risk-averse managers and teams lacking conviction. This tepid behavior is fostered by organizational cultures that are intolerant of dissidents. There are also instances where individuals with positional, expert, or charismatic power may force group members into reluctant consensus. The facade of a team's unified front often takes precedence over making the best decisions.

Each chapter ends with a handful of contra maxims intended to reflect more of the truth seen in management practice. These contra maxims are not meant to be epigrammatic taunts aimed at their semantic brethren, but are merely reflective of more evidentiary thinking. Furthermore, the list of flawed management maxims presented in this volume, as well as those discussed in Volume One, is by no means complete. In the interest of time and space, I have left several maxims alone and will tackle them in subsequent volumes.

My criticism of the aforementioned maxims is evidence based whenever possible. Scholars endeavor to use sound scientific methods when studying management phenomena, mostly accomplished through observation of behavior and the analysis of historical data. While management scholars do not always have the luxury of highly controllable experiments like their counterparts in the more concrete sciences, the management field is filled with talented professionals eager to know the truth. As the author and astronomer Carl Sagan wrote, "Science is based on experiment, on a willingness to challenge old dogma, on an openness to see the universe as it really is. Accordingly, science sometimes requires courage—at the very least the courage to question the conventional wisdom."[2] It is precisely that questioning of conventional wisdom that embodies the fundamental purpose of this book.

Notes

1. Thomas Paine, *Common Sense* (New York, NY: Prometheus, 1995), xi.
2. Carl Sagan, *Broca's Brain: Reflections on the Romance of Science* (New York, NY: Random House, 1979), 16.

Acknowledgements

The spirit of evidentiary criticism conveyed in these pages has been influenced by hundreds of authors and their works. A handful of contemporary books stand out, including: Phil Rosenzweig's *Halo Effect and Eight Other Business Delusions that Deceive Managers*; Jeffrey Pfeffer's and Robert Sutton's *Hard Facts, Dangerous Half-truths and Total Nonsense*; Pfeffer's *Leadership BS*; Thomas Sowell's *Economic Facts and Fallacies*; Scott Shane's *Illusions of Entrepreneurship*; and *Freakonomics* by Steven Levitt and Stephen Dubner. Needless to say I highly recommend these authors and books, for each in their own way dares to call out commonly accepted yet flawed thinking.

I have used empirical evidence, original scholarship, findings from other scholars, the occasional anecdote, and thoughtful opinions of numerous experts to help communicate my positions. My charge has been to provide a critical examination of common maxims that are improperly viewed as universal truths. I encourage critical thinking and welcome a spirited dialogue related to the content in these pages. Furthermore, my criticism is mindful of how difficult it is to execute in many management situations.

I am thankful to several people for their candid reviews and critiques of early concepts and draft chapters. These thoughtful colleagues and friends include Len Deneault, David Castle, Ray McArdle, Thomas Grover, Curtis Lintvedt, Karen Spohn, and Bob Vartabedian. All of these readers are busy professionals, yet they took time to help me work through and refine the manuscript. I will always remember their generosity.

I have benefited from the assistance of several colleagues in the Division of Business at Rivier University, including Amir Toosi, Susan Farina, Chari Henry-Wilson, and James Hussey. As a lifelong fan of libraries and their staffs, I would be remiss not to mention the assistance I received from these remarkable institutions and the professionals that serve them. I am thankful to the staff at Rivier's Regina Library, especially

Holly Klump for her diligent efforts with interlibrary loans, and Alan Witt for his work in acquisitions related to my needs. The staffs of the Pollard Memorial Library, the Merrimack Valley Library Consortium, and Harvard University's Widener Library have also been helpful and responsive. It should be noted that any errors in this book—be they with regard to grammar, syntax, data, or attributions—are mine and mine alone. My personal opinions expressed in this book do not necessarily reflect the beliefs of any of the fine people or organizations that have assisted me.

I subjected many of my former students to draft chapters, and I am grateful for the feedback in their reflective essays and in-class discussions. Additionally, since many of my positions in this work have been ruminating for several years, I am grateful to past co-workers and superiors that I have learned from—of which there are far too many to name.

It has been a pleasure working with everyone at Business Expert Press and S4Carlisle. From editing to production, the entire team helped make the final stages of the project a smooth and rewarding experience.

Lastly, there are many ups, downs, and late nights involved in this type of project. I have been fortunate to count on my wife, Leanne, for her support and encouragement throughout this long process. For all that and more, I am most grateful.

CHAPTER 1

Mission Statement
is a Must for Survival

*Mission statements are among the most blatant and common means
that organizations use to substitute talk for action.*
> —Jeffrey Pfeffer and Robert Sutton, *The Knowledge-doing
> Gap: How Smart Companies Turn Knowledge Into Action*

Know thyself.
> —Ancient Greek inscription, forecourt of Delphi Oracle

A widely held belief is that every organization, large and small, must have a mission statement. Conventional business wisdom tells us that success will elude an organization without a well-articulated beacon of prose to guide it forward. How else are employees, customers, investors, community stakeholders, media outlets, and suppliers supposed to know what business you are in without a clearly defined mission statement? How could your firm face the day and its inevitable uncertainties without a framed, needlepointed statement of purpose hanging on the lobby wall, or a highlighted *raison d'être* easily queried on the About Us page on the company website? The truth is that if your organization's employees need to look at a poster or business card B-side to get direction and motivation, your organization is in big trouble.

In reality, the mission statement is not the indispensable communication tool we've believed it to be for so many years. I'll bet the majority of people that have taken college business courses were told by professors and textbooks that a mission statement is critical to the success of any enterprise. How can you have a strategy without a mission? You have to start with a mission, right?

Wrong! But before we get too far ahead of ourselves, let's review some well-respected and time-honored definitions of this beloved corporate mainstay. Mission statements have primarily been looked upon as indicators of organizational direction and purpose. The iconic management guru Peter Drucker succinctly claimed that when employed, mission statements should answer the following questions: What business are we in? And, what are we trying to achieve?[1] The venerable strategist Henry Mintzberg noted that a mission statement "describes the organization's basic function in society, in terms of the products and services it produces for its customers."[2] Simple enough.

Strategy scholar Jay Barney looks at a firm's mission simply as "its long-term purpose" and the impetus for the strategic management process.[3] One can argue, however, that the mission may be developed *after* a strategic analysis of the firm's capabilities and discovery of opportunities. The latter scenario tends to be more emergent and opportunistic than the former.

Others prefer a more comprehensive definition consisting of eight suggested tenets, including target customers, products, geographic domain, core technologies, commitment to growth and profits, philosophical elements, self-concept, and desired public image.[4] Still another definition captures the common parlance of contemporary mission statements as, "It [mission statement] describes the firm's product, market, and technological areas of emphasis, and it does so in a way that reflects the values and priorities of the firm's strategic decision makers."[5]

Although there is no universally accepted definition for a mission statement, the last of the preceding examples will likely pass the sniff test from most corporate leaders and academics. Although I prefer the simplicity of the legendary Drucker, most agree the mission statement should be an informative descriptor of what kind of organization you are (e.g., What markets do you participate in?) with a sprinkling of some high ranking position or objective (e.g., world leader, most respected, or #1 market share). I'll provide examples later in the chapter that are very descriptive as well as others that will leave you clueless. I'll also include examples of wildly successful firms that do not subscribe to the ethos-building powers of the exalted mission statement. Contrary to the textbooks and popular opinion, there are dozens of blue chip firms that have been immensely successful while seemingly on a rudderless mission to nowhere!

First, I'll briefly review a representative batch of research and facts from the mission, strategy, and corporate communications literature. In particular, we'll look at studies ambitiously attempting to find statistically significant links between mission statement content and organizational performance. This research discussion is by no means comprehensive due to the hundreds of studies completed. My goal here is to provide a brief and balanced accounting of the research. I'll then offer findings and analysis from my own data collection of all the firms in the Standard & Poor's (S&P) 100 and Fortune 500. And for a little fun, a short quiz is provided for those of you wanting to test your mission statement aptitude.

As you read on, ponder the following questions: Do you think the contemporary corporate mission statement is an explicit, short-hand manifesto of the firm? Or, is it simply unnecessary, bemused corporate speak? Is it somewhere in between? I contend that the ubiquitous and sanctimonious maxim spouting that a *Mission statement is a must for survival* is patently untrue. Business has few absolutes, and this overhyped maxim is not one of them.

Perspectives from Mission Research

Despite involving a straightforward communication device, the mission statement research domain has been a lively and controversial area for academic researchers and practitioners alike. Research, including my own work, indicates that statements of mission do not exist in many organizations and are inadequate in others. One study suggested that mission statements are often "merely window dressing."[6]

Noted mission statement researcher Christopher Bart questioned the credibility and usefulness of mission statements, but praised these hopeful objectives:

> the power of mission statements rests in their ability to achieve two key results: (1) to inspire and motivate organizational members to exceptional performance — that is, to influence behavior; and (2) to guide the resource allocation process in a manner that produces consistency and focus.[7]

Bart surmised that managers are either using their mission statements for purposes other than motivation and resource allocation, or are simply unaware of the benefits that can accrue from pursuing these two purposes. This mission statement proponent ultimately concluded that mission statements have the potential to be the "*elan vital* of corporate life."[8] However, Bart warned that misuse of this planning and communication tool occurs frequently and breeds cynicism. My take is that missions are more often ignored, viewed as symbols of hypocrisy and political correctness, or used to co-opt stakeholder opinions.

Citing a research stream that has produced either "no link" or "weak support" for the mission statement-performance dynamic, a researcher in Holland described the lack of empirical evidence on this relationship as "surprising" and "embarrassing." Published in the *European Management Journal*, a study of 38 Dutch multimedia firms revealed a link between mission statements and performance (measured loosely by sales growth vis-a-vis competitors). While this Dutch study began with healthy skepticism, it concluded with a lethargic compromise (i.e., "probably too early to relegate mission statements to the shelf") as well as a more positive finding of, "A mission statement can lead to superior performance." The study also claimed that the more comprehensive the mission statement content, the better the performance. Notably, this study acknowledged the lack of uniformity for terminology in the mission domain among academics and practitioners in the field.[9]

This Dutch study was flawed by a casually operationalized dependent variable (*perception* of relative sales growth) as well as a small sample size. While the researcher asked good questions, it's hard to fathom how the performance outcomes of professional firms can be so influenced by a few generic sentences containing some keywords. Many of these keywords do not have shared meanings across an organization.

Researchers from Old Dominion University (ODU) queried the websites of the 30 largest European, Japanese, and American firms listed in the Fortune Global 500. They were only able to find 22, 15, and 19 mission statements, respectively, from the 30 queries per continent or country. This noncompliance is indicative of the traditional mission statement's lack of importance. In their study, the ODU team looked at mission statement quality (i.e., inclusion of stakeholders, components, and objectives) and their relationship with financial performance. They did find that the inclusion of employee concern, social responsibility and corporate values had positive relationships with financial performance. However, they concluded the bulk of their findings "cast doubt on the notion that firms should develop comprehensive mission statements."[10]

As a by-product of environmental awareness and stewardship, corporate social responsibility (CSR) has gained much traction within corporate communications protocols. The rise of CSR is emblematic of firms being held accountable to stakeholders other than shareholders. Gone are the days of the late Harvard economist Milton Friedman declaring that corporations should be strictly beholden to shareholders, provided they obey the law, of course.

The mission statement has been a prime communications vehicle for firms to publically disseminate their social responsibility initiatives. One study suggested parallels between everyday family values and those that organizations should exhibit. This same research stated that an organization's mission statement guides the development of the organization's desired ethical profile, and this profile is a projection to external publics with whom the organization interacts.[11] Consequently, CSR demands can lead to denser (i.e., higher word count) mission statements that pivot toward a more politically correct and public relations orientation.

A study published in *Corporate Reputation Review* analyzed the top 100 retailers in the United States for the purpose of discovering the context in which CSR was being addressed. The study reported that 20 percent of retailers presented CSR statements on their websites separate from their mission statements; 38 percent had CSR principles embedded in their general mission statements; and 42 percent did not present CSR principles at all on their web pages. The study authors also found that 36 of the non-CSR related mission statements had instead emphasized economic language or used wording that was more philanthropic in nature.[12]

Researchers in Spain examined the mission statements and sustainability reports of 52 Spanish listed firms. The authors suggested that a clearly defined mission statement is capable of influencing a firm's performance because it affects the behavior of employees. The study claimed that companies whose mission and vision are committed to the satisfaction of their stakeholders offer more and better sustainability information than those that are purely shareholder oriented.[13] Again, one cannot help but doubt that employee behavior would significantly impact firm performance because of some language buried so deep in the corporate website that most employees would have trouble finding it.

The nonprofit sector offers an interesting segment for the examination of mission statement relevance. A study of 138 women's rights organizations looked at the relationship of mission statements and financial performance (measured as overhead ratios and growth of contributions). Statistical relationships were so weak that authors concluded that common assumptions about nonprofit mission statements are not necessarily correct. The researchers did, however, comment on the challenges and nuances of nonprofit mission statements by revealing that "In the case of the non-profit organization, the variety of distinct constituencies complicates effectiveness measurement even more, because each constituency could have its own preferences for organizational outcomes."[14]

This last example illustrates how mission statements can fall short when trying to serve too many masters. In the end, missions often mutate into instruments of affectation and stakeholder appeasement.

Blue Chips: Got Mission?

Being included in an S&P index is a remarkable achievement for publically traded firms in the United States. The S&P indexes have what you may consider to be a *no slackers rule*. All these firms are referred to as blue chip companies, although the term is sometimes used to connote current denizens of the Dow Jones Industrial Average. Successful track records in profitability, shareholder returns, and market capitalization help sustain a firm's place in the indexes. Mostly, these firms are legitimate, trusted names with staying power. No overnight successes or one-hit wonders.

My research for the S&P 100 firms was conducted in 2011. I used the Fortune 500 database for similar purposes in 2015. The methodology for collecting acceptable mission statements included the following protocol, in order: review the company's annual report; check company website; and finally, telephonically contact company personnel (e.g., public relations or investor relations). For the S&P 100, 75 mission statements were culled from the 100 companies in the pool, yielding a significant 25 percent of firms with no mission statement![15]

For the larger data set using the 2014 Fortune 500 list of firms, we found 98 firms (19.6 percent) void of mission statements. Given that roughly 20 to 25 percent of blue chip companies do not have mission statements, it appears that a mission statement is not necessary for organizational survival. Furthermore, it seems that the mission statement is not required for above average performance in terms of revenue and earnings. This finding complements previous academic research that has failed to show convincing relationships (either with cause-and-effect explanatory power or simple correlations) that support the mission-performance proposition. The evidence presents a weak case for a mission statement mandate.

Given that these samples contained many of the largest and most profitable firms in the United Sates, we found it odd that our telephone contact with various company personnel often revealed a lack of understanding or recollection of the company's mission statement. Again, while some mission statements were very prominent in annual reports, company websites or lobby walls, a surprising degree of difficulty was encountered trying to determine the existence of mission statements in these samples.

Numerous companies do not use the mission statement moniker even though their company credos fit the most comprehensive of the term's varied definitions. The subjectivity of what is and what isn't a mission statement is a problematic research limitation in this field. While I don't have specific data to back this up, I believe the adoption rate of *missionlike* statements is growing, yet use of the formal and descriptive label *mission statement* is declining. Terms such as *vision* and *statement of purpose* have superseded mission, I believe, because missions are looked upon as more finite, concrete endeavors that occasionally end in failure. Missions are intended to be accomplished and reflect accountability. Contrastingly, vision statements, statements of values, company philosophies, and other gobbledygook of this ilk are more grandiose, idealistic, and generic in nature. We are more forgiving of the less tangible and conceptual proclamations that don't come to fruition. For example, let's say you didn't quite cure that disease or fully realize that vision of daily flights to Mars. That's OK, after all, those were pretty lofty, aspirational dreams.

Word Play

Since language style and word choice can dramatically alter the intent of corporate communications (and make mission statements hard to find), I'd like to review some results of my research using content analysis methodology on mission statements. Content analysis is simply the computerized search of keywords or their variants within chosen text.

I performed content analysis on the 75 mission statements found in the 2011 listing of S&P 100 firms. Table 1.1 includes a list of 15 words queried along with their corresponding frequencies (percentage of mission statements in which the term appears).

Not surprisingly, keywords *customer* (48 percent) and *innovation* (19 percent) were recorded at relatively high incidences.[16] However, my finding for the term *customer* is much lower than the incidence of 68 percent reported in a comparable study published the prior year in the

Table 1.1 Mission statement keywords and frequencies

Keyword (or some variation thereof)	Frequency
Customer	48%
Service	20%
Innovation	19%
Provide	15%
Lead	13%
Global	13%
Best	12%
Health	12%
Quality	12%
Develop	11%
Strive	10%
Technology	10%
Environment	8%
Sustainability	6%
Responsibility	6%

Academy of Strategic Management Journal.[17] Also, a study focused on mission statement content of 50 international airlines revealed a still higher incidence of the keyword customer (72 percent). The reason for these higher frequencies is likely due to a much more liberal interpretation of what constitutes a mission statement. For instance, my review of the airline sample and three of its more dense mission statements revealed word counts of 153, 159, and 205 words.[18] In the study I conducted on the S&P 100, the inclusion criteria for valid mission statements were much more parsimonious. It is no wonder that there will be higher frequencies of selected words from content analysis queries given such voluminous statements.

Related to so-called mission statement *quality* and *effectiveness*, I conducted a survey to see how identifiable mission statements were to their firms' respective S&P industry classification (e.g., financial, consumer discretionary, and health care). In short, do the mission statements inform the reader of the most basic tenet of the mission definition: What type of work or sector is the firm engaged?

I prepped 57 respondents with a descriptive list of the S&P categories but blinded the respondents to the names of the firms. They were provided mission statements and instructed to guess the S&P category of the firms. Only 37 percent of the mission statements were correctly identified by at least 50 percent of respondents. A similar number (40 percent) of the total individual responses were correct.[19] A for-profit mission statement is often a poor performer in terms of conveying the industry in which the firm competes. But if the mission statement is meant to communicate politically correct or socially oriented meanings, then these statements generally have more merit.

Why were nearly two-thirds of blue chip company mission statements incorrectly identified in our survey? Perhaps confusion ensues from misleading words, such as Capital One's mission being wrongly attributed to the health care sector due to the use of "healthy communities" in the firm's mission statement. Contrastingly and thanks to strong branding efforts, Capitol One (as a firm's name) is widely known as a financial sector company. Additionally, Walmart's mission, "Our mission is to help people save money so they can live better," was frequently misidentified as a financial sector company instead of a consumer staples concern.

While the domain of for-profit industrial firms may not present the most descriptive mission statements, other domains may be better suited for identifiability. For instance, one study of the missions for accredited colleges of business found 94 percent of 408 institutions sampled had sufficiently articulated their primary product.[20] This high rate of compliance is likely due to specific accreditation standards that require member schools to adhere to specific assessments regarding mission orientation. In other words, mission statement adoption may be a result of an external mandate that legitimizes, in part, the operations of member institutions. Obviously, the universe of for-profit public firms (not engaged in higher education) has no such formal edict.

Two problems arise when comparing results such as those just mentioned. The first is the lack of uniformity regarding what qualifies as a mission-related declaration. Are statements of values, or purpose, or vision appropriate as proxies for mission? Does it depend on what is communicated regardless of the label used? For example, the aerospace behemoth Boeing does not have a formal mission statement per se, but has a vision statement that reads and smells like a mission statement. A 2008 study published in the *Journal of Business Communication* identified mission statements in 91.3 percent (42 of 46 firms) in a Fortune 1000 sample, yet only 38.1 percent (16 of 46) actually labeled the corporate text in question as a mission.[21] This ambiguity with terminology lends credence to my argument that mission statements are largely corporate word fluff and not truly rule-based. Mission determination is often a subjective scavenger hunt for anyone attempting to ascertain the mission of a firm. But again, a properly executed corporate communications program, integrated branding effort, packaging scheme, and signs on the firms' vans should suffice to satisfy most stakeholders' curiosities. Not surprisingly, we found mission statements to be puzzling even when asking company personnel. Some employees seemed embarrassed that they didn't know the official company mission—even when their firm didn't have one!

The second problem lies with the lack of will from academic researchers and corporations to face the truth regarding the utility of mission statements. We've covered the issue of weak links between missions and performance. But we continue to look past the lack of face validity that missions have with regard to performance and signaling (i.e., telling the uninitiated what the firm is, does, or seeks). Are organizations such a mystery (with their minions toiling away in hidden underground lairs) that reasonably intelligent community members, employees, customers, and potential investors need to inquire as to what the mission statements are? Sadly, thanks to so much corporate mumbo jumbo and legalese, you may know *less* about a company *after* you read its mission statement.

Time for a Pop Quiz

How about testing your corporate know-how with a short mission statement quiz? Listed below are the mission statements of 10 well-known firms. Your mission, if you choose to accept it, is to match the mission statement with the firms listed beneath the quiz. And yes there are a few more firms than mission statements, sorry. I have included mostly brief statements of mission to spare you the dread of reading some of the more long-winded corporate propaganda. Check your performance against the answer key provided at the end of the chapter. Good luck!

	Mission statement	Name of firm
1.	Our mission is to work hard, have fun, and make money by providing legendary service and great products at everyday low prices.	_____
2.	Our mission is to become change agents and innovators—using [BLANK] Lean Six Sigma to constantly search for a better way to meet our customers' challenges and to create business process outsourcing, IT solutions, new technologies, products, and services for world class commercial and government clients that enable better results.	_____
3.	To treat others as we would like to be treated.	_____
4.	Be the safest, most customer-focused, and successful transportation company in the world.	_____
5.	Every day, everywhere, we use our technology and expertise to make payments safe, simple, and smart.	_____
6.	To champion every client's goals with passion and integrity.	_____
7.	To continually provide our members with quality goods and services at the lowest possible prices.	_____

8.	[Blank] will produce superior financial returns for its share owners by providing high value-added logistics, transportation, and related business service through focused operating companies. Customer requirements will be met in the highest quality manner appropriate to each market segment served. [Blank] will strive to develop mutually rewarding relationships with its employees, partners, and suppliers. Safety will be the first consideration in all operations. Corporate activities will be conducted to the highest ethical and professional standards.	_____
9.	Serving others: For Customers... a better life. For shareholders... a superior return. For Employees... respect and opportunity.	_____
10	Bring inspiration and innovation to every athlete in the world.	_____

List of firms for above quiz:

A. Fed Ex	B. Sherwin-Williams	C. Xerox	D. Dollar General
E. Nike	F. Bank of America	G. Dow Chemical	H. Charles Schwab
I. MasterCard	J. J.C. Penney	K. Costco Wholesale	L. Tractor Supply
M. General Electric	N. Apple	O. Medtronic	P. Norfolk Southern

Some of the mission statements in the quiz were easy to match, especially if they mentioned what business they were in. A few were quirky and didn't give much detail, while a couple were of the wordy variety that provided way too much information (lots of public relations jargon, input from the legal team, e.g., "safety"). Note the firms listed are very well known, and hardly need a mission to explain what they are all about thanks to strong branding, performance, and market clout.

I won't give away the answers to the above exercise, but I will tell you the names of some well-known firms that *do not* have mission statements. They include Apple, General Electric, Best Buy, Delta Airline, Time Warner, CBS, Baxter International, Kinder Morgan, Textron, State Street Corp, Ralph Lauren, Sherwin-Williams, and Wynn Resorts.

Given the absence of a formal mission for many successful firms, and a hodgepodge of inconsistent jargon used to describe corporate intentions, it's easy to disavow the maxim of *Mission statement is a must for survival*. Far from being an absolute, this faux maxim still has many believers yet scant evidence exists to support its currency. How do we explain excellence and strong performance among companies that do not outwardly declare robust, academically correct mission statements? Also, why are many eloquent missions so difficult to find given their alleged duty to inform and inspire?

Many successful leaders and entrepreneurs believe it is a necessity to have everyone in the organization buy into the mission. Forgive my clichés, but the mission is commonly purported to get *everyone on the same song sheet* or *rowing in the same direction*. And yes, I think a shared purpose can be useful. But my point is that you can have a collective fire in the belly or esprit de corps across the firm *without* the formal statement. In fact, I posit that the overformalization of a mission statement may be detrimental to the overall effort of the organization. The mission may become too rigid, corny, and cliché. Mission allegiance may impede mission emergence. Left unchecked, the mission statement could transform into a bureaucratic rabbit hole, leading to numbing compliance and a disabling of innovation and risk taking.

Employees at Google, for instance, have known for years that they are tasked with leading the world in search. Innovators at the Google's X Division (i.e., Google Glass, self-driving cars, and so on) know they are charged with devising paradigm-shifting breakthroughs. Google's programmers don't need a mission-related tattoo on their arm to motivate or remind them to improve search algorithms or increase paid search revenue. For the record, prior to the Alphabet restructuring, the mothership mission statement for Google was an elegantly concise, "To organize the world's information and make it universally accessible and useful." Short and sweet.

Reliance on statements of mission may mask serious execution problems within organizations. Employees should implicitly know the organization's short- to intermediate-term purpose via updates from management, annual reports, meetings, their own performance evaluations, hallway chitchat, public relations, and seeing what is being shipped out to customers. Consistent and respectful communication throughout the organization sets the stage for expectations regarding direction and performance. If employees, customers, or investors need a mission statement to define the company, something is very wrong.

Case of the Wild Winged Buffalo: Mission Versus Slogan

For a final example, take a look below at the mission statement for Buffalo Wild Wings, Inc., (a.k.a. B-Dubs®) a national chain of sports bars/restaurants. On the plus side, the mission is upbeat, motivational for the employees, mentions that they serve food, and indicates the firm values financial performance. Incidentally, employee motivation is important at B-Dubs since the workforce is relatively young with much of the staff having limited work experience.[22] On the not so positive side, the mission statement is long-winded (116 words) and contains lots of information better suited for public relations flyers, the break room bulletin board, and general announcements at preshift quality meetings. Here's the formal proclamation:

At Buffalo Wild Wings our mission is clearly defined:

> Our mission is to WOW people every day!
>
> *We are guest-driven*
> *We will WOW our guests every day by achieving the highest level of satisfaction with an extraordinary focus on friendly service, food, fun and value.*
>
> *We are team-focused*
> *We will WOW our team members by providing the same respect, positive encouragement and fair treatment within the organization that we expect Team Members to share externally with every guest.*
>
> *We are community-connected*
> *We will WOW the communities where we do business by practicing good citizenship and helping to make these communities better places to live, work and grow.*
>
> *We are dedicated to excellence*
> *We will WOW our stakeholders with outstanding, industry-leading financial results and operational performance.*[23]

Now, contrast the above mission statement with B-Dubs' more commonly known promotional slogan that tells you pretty much all you need to know in three words:

Wings. Beer. Sports.™

Wow! Given the choice between the mission and the slogan, I vote for the slogan. Three words capture the company's essence and customer experience better than the 116 words in the mission statement. The slogan succinctly tells you what business they are in. One can assume from the slogan that this is not a philanthropic organization, and we can further assume that their objective is not to lose money. The slogan may not point toward a vision-quested intergalactic future, espouse market dominance, or wallow in political correctness and CSR, but it tells a good story in just three syllables.

This elegant simplicity is no mystery to the B-Dubs, Inc. brain trust either. While the aforementioned mission statement was found buried in a franchisee employment solicitation, the promotional slogan was prominently displayed under their About Us tab and elaborated on as follows:

> But really, all you need to know "About Us" is these three things: Wings. Beer. Sports.™ Why do those three things matter to us so much? Because that's what our fans want, and that's what we're all about—making our fans happy.[24]

Finally, some corporate communication that makes sense. Come to think of it, just seeing the logo or the brand name tells me what goes on inside one of their establishments, mostly because they have a marketing communications program that is well-executed. As for B-Dubs' long-term performance prospects, only time and execution proficiency will tell in the end. But it's hard to fathom how having a mission statement (of any kind) is going to help predict if a company thrives, fails, or merely survives for 10 or 20 years.

Contra Maxims for Mission Statements

Mission statements are not necessary. Mission statements should be informative only to the uninitiated. Missions should be known implicitly due to a multitude of other indicators. Mission allegiance may impede mission emergence. Strategic objectives matter more than mission statements. Lastly, if you rely on a mission statement to motivate employees, attract customers, or woo investors, you are in big trouble!

Answers *to the mission statement quiz are as follows:*

1. (L) Tractor Supply 2. (C) Xerox 3. (J) J.C. Penney 4. (P) Norfolk Southern 5. (I) MasterCard 6. (H) Charles Schwab 7. (K) Costco Wholesale 8. (A) Fed Ex 9. (D) Dollar General 10. (E) Nike

Mission Quiz Score Interpretation

All 10 Correct: Mission savant. Seek help immediately.
7–9 Correct: Corporate communications wonk. Congratulations, maybe.
4–6 Correct: Overthinker or average guesser.
0–3 Correct: Bad guesser, apathetic, or too literal.

Notes

1. Peter Drucker, *Management: Tasks, Responsibilities, and Practices* (New York, NY: Harper & Row, 1973).
2. Henry Mintzberg, *The Rise and Fall of Strategic Planning* (New York, NY: Prentice Hall, 1994).
3. Jay Barney and William Hesterly, *Strategic Management and Competitive Advantage* (Upper Saddle River, NJ: Prentice Hall, 2010), 5, 24.
4. John Pearce and Fred David, "Corporate Mission Statements: The Bottom Line," *Academy of Management Executive* 1, no. 2 (1987): 109–116.
5. John Pearce and Richard Robinson, *Strategic Management: Formulation, Implementation, and Control, 8th ed.* (New York, NY: McGraw-Hill Education, 2003), 23.
6. Craig Lundberg, "Zero-in: A Technique for Formulating Better Mission Statements," *Business Horizons* 27, no. 5 (1984): 30.
7. Christopher Bart, "Sex, Lies, and Mission Statements," *Business Horizons* 40, no. 6 (1997): 9.

8. Ibid., 17.

9. Jatinder Sidhu, "Mission Statements: Is it Time to Shelve Them?" *European Management Journal* 21, no. 4 (2003): 439–446.

10. Barbara Bartkus, Myron Glassman and Bruce McAfee, "Mission Statement Quality and Financial Performance," *European Management Journal* 24, no. 1 (2006): 86–94.

11. Donald Robin and R. Eric Reidenbach, "Social Responsibility, Ethics, and Marketing Strategy: Closing the Gap Between Concept and Application," *Journal of Marketing* 51, no. 1 (1987): 44–58.

12. Min-Young Lee, Ann Fairhurst, and Scarlett Wesley, "Corporate Social Responsibility: A Review of the Top 100 US Retailers," *Corporate Reputation Review 12*, no. 2 (2009): 140–158.

13. Jose Moneva, Juana Rivera-Lirio, and Maria Muñoz-Torres, "The Corporate Stakeholder Commitment and Social and Financial Performance," *Industrial Management & Data Systems 107, no.* 1 (2007): 84–102.

14. Gary Kirk and Shabnam Beth Nola, "Nonprofit Mission Statement Focus and Financial Performance," *Nonprofit Management & Leadership* 20, no. 4 (2010): 479.

15. Kevin Wayne and James Hussey, "The Contemporary American Mission Statement: Explicit Manifesto or Bemused Corporate Speak," *Conference Proceedings of Northeast Business & Economics Association*, Oct 2012.

16. Ibid.

17. Darwin King, Carl Case and Kathleen Premo, "A Mission Statement Analysis Comparing the United States and Three Other English Speaking Countries," *Academy of Strategic Management Journal* 10, (2011): 21–45.

18. Sharon Kemp and Larry Dwyer, "Mission Statements of International Airlines: A Content Analysis," *Tourism Management* 24, no. 6 (2003): 635–653.

19. Wayne and Hussey, "The Contemporary American Mission Statement"

20. Timothy Palmer and Jeremy Short, "Mission Statements in U.S. Colleges of Business: An Empirical Examination of their Content with Linkages to Configurations and Performance," *Academy of Management Learning & Education* 7, no. 4 (2008): 454–470.

21. Linda Stallworth Williams, "The Mission Statement: A Corporate Reporting Tool with a Past, Present, and Future," *Journal of Business Communication* 45, no. 2 (2008): 94–119.

22. Bloomberg Business, "Buffalo Wild Wings CEO on their Secret Sauce," Interview with CEO Sally Smith, Bloomberg TV, 26 Aug 2015, http://www.bloomberg.com/news/videos/2015-08-26/buffalo -wild-wings-expansion-plan-takes-flight (accessed Aug 29, 2015).

23. Buffalo Wild Wings. Inc., "World Wide Wings: A Franchisee of Buffalo Wild Wings," http://www.buffalowildwingsor.com/default. aspx?Page=About (accessed Aug 29, 2015). Note: B-Dubs is a registered trademark and Wings. Beer. Sports. is a trademark of Buffalo Wild Wings, Inc.

24. Buffalo Wild Wings. Inc., "Our Story," http://www.buffalowildwings. com/en/about/ (accessed Aug 25, 2015).

CHAPTER 2

Learn a Second Language (Other than English)

For last year's words belong to last year's language
And next year's words await another voice.

—T.S. Eliot, *Little Gidding*

The propagation of English is an industry; not a happy accident.
—Henry Hitchings, *The Language Wars: A History of Proper English*

A few years ago I was online reading about territorial disputes in the South China and East China Seas when a nautical photograph caught my eye. The most prominent markings on a Japanese Coast Guard ship were the words (in English) "JAPAN COAST GUARD." Cruising alongside the Japanese vessel was a similarly sized Chinese ship, whose port side was adorned with letters as big as sailors that read: "CHINA MARINE SURVEILLANCE," again in English.[1]

Curious, I searched to see how a coast guard vessel in Vietnam was marked, and sure enough I found an impressive ship labeled as "VIETNAM COAST GUARD." Hmmm.

I should not have been so surprised. The English language is far and away the lingua franca for global business, culture, and international relations. The number of global English speakers is estimated to be over 1.5 billion, which includes those designated with English as a first, second, or foreign language.[2] Additionally, hundreds of millions more are engaged in English language courses. There may be more people speaking English in India than there are native English speakers living in the United States.[3] In a 2015 paper for the Scottish Institute of Research in

Economics, Jacques Melitz reported 63 percent of multinational enterprises conduct their business in English, while another 20 percent use a mixed language model. English also serves as the official language of the Organization of the Petroleum Exporting Countries (OPEC), International Monetary Fund (IMF), World Bank, South Asian Association for Regional Cooperation, and functions as the standard for international air traffic control (i.e., *Airspeak*).[4] Do you copy? Over.

War, natural disasters, trade, travel, international pop culture, literature, music, media, and technology (e.g., radio, television, and Internet) have all contributed to change the world's languages. English has benefited greatly from this dynamism. However, there has been much antipathy toward English as a global tongue.

Americans in particular have been chastised for their lack of multilingualism and weak knowledge of geography. While I will not defend the average American's map reading deficiencies, I do regard the call for native English speakers to learn another language as misguided. This chapter counters the assertion that native English speakers should *learn a second language*. This effort is by no means a gimmick to serve an elitist, nationalistic, or isolationist cause. On the contrary, in-depth knowledge of multiple cultures, as well as proficiency in mathematics and programming languages, would be better investments than learning a second language. There are exceptions, of course, such as specific careers in the State Department, intelligence community, travel and tourism industry, prolonged ex-pat assignments, or perhaps a vocational need to learn the ancient secrets of Italian marble sculpting, for example. And yes, language learning is a big part of cross-cultural immersion. However, it is more advantageous to be globally aware than specifically adept at a second language—unless of course that second language is English. To be clear, for those that do not know English presently, I recommend learning English to at least some functional level.

A Gallup Poll found that 96 percent of Americans believed that immigrants to the United States should learn English. This finding supports one of the competitive strengths of the United States, that of a generally monolingual populace. Widespread adoption of English in the United States is an example where the masses (and their markets) have gotten it right. Nevertheless, that same Gallup Poll revealed 70 percent of Americans thought learning a second language to be "essential" (20 percent) or "important" (50 percent).[5]

I am not alone in my resistance to foreign language learning just to keep up appearances. Writing for the Organization of American Historians, Georgia State's John McMillian bemoans the lingering foreign language requirement of many graduate history programs. He acknowledges English as the "most important language for scholars." McMillian explains the persistence of many academic foreign language requirements as the:

> result of a virus-like phenomenon known as autopoiesis. That is to say, they're based on assumptions, or mind-sets, that became entrenched a very long time ago, and since then have been handed down so frequently as to become the conventional wisdom. Alas, conventional wisdom often elides critical scrutiny—even among history professors.[6]

More reasons are forthcoming, but suffice it to say that English, in all its variations, offers a relatively efficient platform for standardized global communication. A great many of the world's 6,000 or so languages are classified as "peripheral."[7] Unfortunately, marginally utilized languages and dialects will continue to disappear. Local and international efforts are necessary to curate and preserve languages not vibrant enough to sustain themselves.

From Early, Dark Days to the Language of Empire

English derives much of its flavor from conquest, as the tongue of both victor and vanquished. After the Romans had abandoned Celtic Britain, the fifth century brought the invasion of Britain by the Saxons, Angles, and Jutes. These Germanic tribes hailed from present day Holland (formerly Friesland), Germany, and Denmark.[8] Many of the roots of English begin here, mixing with Latin, although few but scholars and clergy did or would speak the language of old school Roman Catholicism.

Danish Vikings would invade in the late 8th century, bringing with them some Old Norse vocabulary at the point of a spear. While it looked as though Old English would be wiped out, Alfred the Great saved the island from Viking dominance with a victory at Wessex in 878 AD.[9] Next, it was William the Conqueror's turn as Normans from the European mainland began a 300-year occupation after winning the Battle of Hastings in 1066. The Norman Conquest brought with it new linguistic contributions. Old English would become Middle English in the shadows of Old French-speaking governance.

In 1348, the Black Plague began devastating Britain. Ironically, this scourge had a bright side for English: killing off many communal, Latin-speaking clergy and Normans. With so many of the population gone, there were economic opportunities for the surviving speakers of Old English. Meanwhile, the Norman homeland was lost to France, so even the ruling class started to mix in more with the locals in Britain, further enriching the language.[10] What did not kill Old English certainly made it stronger.

The Renaissance, improved navigation capabilities, and colonial aspirations brought flourishing international trade. Shakespeare's plays and sonnets dazzled audiences throughout the late 16th and early 17th centuries. British military might and colonialism helped spread England's two greatest exports: English and Shakespeare. During the 18th and 19th centuries, English gained its foothold in the Caribbean, the American colonies, India, Hong Kong, and Australia. To this day English unites much of India, given the subcontinent's myriad of regional languages and dialects. The English language essentially had a first mover advantage in terms of modern international trade.

The ascension of America's global clout, particularly at the beginning of the 20th century, was another boost for English. Victory in both World Wars (WWs), the post-WWII Marshall Plan's contribution to rebuilding Europe, the founding of the United Nations in New York, and economic dominance at mid-century all bolstered the impact of the English language and American culture worldwide.

Hollywood's Supporting Role

The rise of Hollywood as a productive cluster of film making and exporting was an important 20th-century contribution to the global reach of English. Hollywood dominated the global film industry in the silent era, aided by the big studio system and its production prowess. The advent of the talkies in the late 1920s and throughout the 1930s initially sparked national cinema in much of Europe. However, a paradox arose. Tyler Cowen, professor of economics at George Mason University, writes:

> The talkies, by introducing issues of translation, boosted the dominant world language of English and thus benefited Hollywood. Given the growing importance of English as a world language, and the focal importance of the United States, European countries would sooner import films from Hollywood than from each other.[11]

Counterintuitively, non-English film production soared in Europe, but these films were poorly positioned for exporting. Many Hollywood executives viewed the disruptive technology of sound not as a threat but as an opportunity. Sound helped make motion picture production and theater viewing more expensive. The American film industry, with its larger economies of scale, was ideally suited for this seismic shift in film making.[12]

The market advantage and dominance of English language films became a "self-reinforcing" standard. Even film exports from the United Kingdom grew sharply, with global successes including *Lawrence of Arabia*, *The Bridge on the River Kwai* and, of course, the still popular *James Bond* series.[13] Indian film icon Kamal Haasan sees English as a cultural and strategic imperative. Haasan's optimism for the future of India's film industry, with English as a key source of leverage, is apparent from his recent comments:

> It's time India started making its films in the language that it communicates in — interstate communication. It is not done in the Kannada [language] between Tamil Nadu and Karnataka [adjacent states with different spoken languages]. Interstate communication between Maharashtra [state] and Tamil Nadu happens because we have one national language — called English. So that is our strength and we should start making films in that language.[14]

English as Global Standard for Business

Although European Union (EU) members represent 24 languages, this formidable trading bloc conducts most of its parliamentary affairs in English.[15] A growing cadre of multinational firms has adopted English as their standard language, including South Korea's Samsung, Japan's e-commerce giant Rakuten, French automaker Renault, and the European consortium's Airbus.[16] For international business, English falls under two main acronyms: ELF (English as Lingua Franca) and BELF (Business English as Lingua Franca). While both are commonly used, BELF designates the term more specifically for use in international business. More recently, some scholars have begun to use the BELF acronym to mean English as Business Lingua Franca to denote "the domain of use rather than the type of English."[17] A third acronym, EIB (English for International Business), is also employed by researchers.[18]

Tsedal Neeley of Harvard Business School sees many strategic benefits from a common corporate language for multinational corporations (MNCs). Neeley believes MNCs could be at a competitive disadvantage without a common language. She views global coordination of tasks and resources, along with the capacity to excel in negotiations and merger and acquisition activities as key reasons to be united with one language for business.[19]

Neeley stresses that if not managed properly, there can be morale problems between native and non-native speakers. All employees need to buy in to the larger goals supported by standardized language. However, if an individual's English skills are weak, he may lose confidence and not contribute. In a qualitative study of a French technology firm using English as a common language, Neeley discovered varying degrees of anxiety with nonnative English speakers depending on their self-perceived English proficiency. This is especially damaging in terms of not speaking up when there are problems, such as a design flaw or safety issue. Furthermore, observations at this French firm revealed that non-native English speakers "shared a common attitude of resentment and distrust toward their native English-speaking coworkers."[20]

A company utilizing a global supply chain has to rely on good communication. Sourcing components, testing, and assembly from all over the world are hard enough under ideal conditions. Add muddled or hesitant communication to the mix and the result is an ineffective supply chain. Harvard's Neeley cautions not to let language fluency substitute for cultural fluency, skills, or talent.[21] Too many international customer service managers, for example, have been hired for their multilingualism only to be discovered later as ineffective with customers, budgets, or leading subordinates.

In an attempt to ascertain what barriers most inhibited MNC-team functioning and knowledge seeking, the Wharton School's Martine Haas and Duke's Jonathon Cummings studied over 2,000 members of 289 teams working in a large agricultural products firm. Differences (e.g., potential barriers) within teams were geographic, nationality (including native language), structural (e.g., functional area and business unit), and demographic. Surprisingly, the biggest barriers to team communication were geographic and structural. Nationality and demographics were not found to be so important. Sixty-seven different countries of birth were reported among the 2,090 respondents.[22] This MNC uses English as an official language, which in addition to making data collection easier for researchers, likely mitigates communication and knowledge-seeking barriers among team members of varying national origins.

A large German MNC with operations in 25 countries was the subject of a multimethod study delving into the use of English as a business lingua franca. Meetings, telephone conferences, dinners, and interviews were used to determine language usage. While German was deemed unacceptable for cross-cultural use, researchers observed native speakers reverting to German once they realized all non-German speakers left the immediate area. This finding mirrors my own experience on business trips to Germany and France. The study author stressed BELF should not attempt to mimic native English, but rather serve as an "international contract language—[bringing] together nonnative as well as native Englishes from various linguacultural backgrounds spoken with varying degrees of proficiency."[23]

Another German MNC with English as a corporate requirement was the subject of an ethnographic study of nearly 100 globally distributed employees. These employees belonged to several software development teams. Published in the *Journal of International Business Studies*, this paper indicated that power imbalances could exacerbate language differences as a barrier to coordination. Researchers found "communication anxieties and frustration . . . from the use of English as the lingua franca."[24]

Importantly, this study posits that "Language may be more salient and explosive than nationality, which can go unnoticed when there is a strong occupational culture, or when distance renders some of these differences less visible."[25] Work teams—especially when geographically dispersed—are inherently plagued by coordination and cooperation issues regardless of language differences. For instance, team members located on different floors or adjacent buildings can seem as though they are thousands of miles away depending on team dynamics. However, it is logical to assume that language-related problems on conference calls or e-mails will manifest themselves more often than issues of geography or nationality.

The Swiss company EF Education First Ltd. publishes an English Proficiency Index for Companies (EPI-c) report to serve as a benchmark for workforce English proficiency. Industries scoring high in workforce English include consulting and legal services while countries ranking high include Denmark, Netherlands, Sweden, and Norway. Industries not performing well in the EPI-c are more local in nature, such as manufacturing, construction, food, beverage, and tobacco. Countries with poor rankings include Saudi Arabia, Panama, and Mexico. The report contends poorly ranked countries in the EPI-c will face difficult competitive pressures as globalization continues to intensify.[26]

An interesting paper from Finland looked at the language dynamics resulting from mergers between Swedish and Finnish firms. While English has recently become the intercultural lingua franca among Scandinavian countries, traditionally it was Swedish, or "rather a variant usually referred to as 'Scandinavian,' which is a fluid combination of Swedish, Norwegian, Danish, and Icelandic."[27] Note that Finnish does not have the commonalities shared by the aforementioned languages. Finns typically study Swedish in school. A current trend for Pan-Nordic corporations is to adopt English as a corporate language.

Field observations in this study noted the discussion and deliberation tendencies of the Swedes versus the directness and quicker decision making of the Finns.[28] These cultural tendencies color the more neutral foundation of BELF. A "dynamic interactive process" emerges within employee discourse. Postmerger communication challenges are alleviated to some extent by the use of BELF (i.e., at least for many Finns in this case study). Business English per se has no native speakers, non-native speakers nor learners. BELF "merely has business communicators going about their everyday jobs."[29] Nevertheless, participants should be wary of their own and others' cultural presuppositions. Employees should be trained to note the "pragmatic communication aspects of language," implying that their job duties and company goals are of more concern than the language used.[30]

One of the recurring criticisms in the BELF research literature is how English language proficiency provides an unfair status or authority advantage over those less savvy with English. Similarly, this is an unfortunate aspect of the power of communicative talents seen in all-native English work teams. For example, you may have witnessed coworkers that appear confident, talk a great game, and seem to have a command of an issue or problem. They are the same people that interview well given their accomplished interpersonal and communication skills. However, after the smoke clears and you think about what solutions or actual work is produced by these types, you may be left wanting for tangible contributions. Often called posers, these Charlatans will superficially thrive wherever communication skills are prized. Thus, the best defense in a non-native English setting is to upgrade the BELF skillset of everyone involved.

Code Talkers

Given today's importance of technology and computing, how does language fare in the digital age? Does artificial intelligence, algorithm construction, or the preponderance of new programming languages threaten the global dominance of English? Thus far no, but. . . .

Writing for the *Harvard Business Review*, Bill Fisher cites the top 10 programming languages, as ranked by Institute of Electrical and Electronics Engineers (IEEE) Spectrum in 2014, as all being in English. Fisher adds that two of the languages, Python and Ruby, were written by native-Dutch and native-Japanese speakers, respectively.[31] W3 Techs, an online content measurement service, pegs English as representing 53.7 percent of all online content. Russian, German, Japanese, and Spanish trail well behind at 6.3, 5.7, 5.0, and 4.9 percent, respectively.[32] A recent *Bloomberg Businessweek* story on smartphone app development described non-English programming languages as niche, and claimed the dominance of English language coding leaves "non-English speakers at a disadvantage."[33]

Given the need for language translation, many wonder if Google Translate will emerge one day as a pragmatic, real-life version of the original *Star Trek's* universal translator. Maybe someday, but for years effective *translation memory* has been able to access large swaths of pre-translated text for quick feedback.[34] A 2016 *Harvard Business Review* piece stressed the limitations of today's translation code and the need for human interpretation. Algorithms have long been knocked (and praised) for their singular, myopic focus, meaning they do exactly what you tell them to do. Algorithms are literal devices, viewed as black boxes since they "don't explain why they offer particular recommendations."[35] Today, they just *do*, but more accomplished algorithms are no doubt coming in the future.

It is sobering to note that tech entrepreneur Elon Musk and Nobel Prize-winning physicist Stephen Hawking have voiced reservations about artificial intelligence. In a *New York Times Magazine* article, the writer Gideon Lewis-Kraus reassures us that machine language still cannot grasp much of the nuance and shades of meaning that colors human language. Computational linguists are not interested in the intricacies of English, Spanish, German, or whatever. They strive for parsimony, to be *close enough*. Lewis-Kraus provides us with a figurative ice bath as he depicts coders of machine translation programs with:

> They see the redundancy and allusiveness of natural languages as
> a matter not of intricacy but of confusion and inefficiency. Most
> valuable utterances revert to the mean of statistical probability. If
> this makes them unpopular with poets and fanciers of language,
> so be it.[36]

Well, so much for flowery adjectives. Nevertheless, I'll likely forgive machine coders in the future if they set me up with a hologram that makes hot cocoa and reads to me before bedtime.

Global Networks

In an attempt to measure the influence of world languages beyond population and economic measures, researchers from multiple universities (led by MIT's Media Lab) constructed global language network (GLN) models to ascertain the global popularity and multilingual connectedness of individual languages. Variables meant to indicate the degree of *multilingual coexpressions* included book translations (to and from each language), multiple language editions of Wikipedia, and multilingual messages on Twitter. Additionally, the number of famous people born in a language's corresponding country also correlated with the models' primary input variables.[37]

English was found to be the dominant hub of the GLNs even while controlling for population size and wealth. Intermediate hubs included Spanish, German, French, Russian, Portuguese, and Chinese. The number of book translations *from* English to other languages was particularly impressive, totaling over five times as many entries as French and German. Interestingly, despite their large population numbers, Chinese, Hindi, and Arabic were seen more as peripheral in graphic terms since they do not link well to distant languages. A lack of multilingual exchange for Arabic, for instance, limits its capacity to serve as a global language hub. The visual mapping demonstrates how the "position of a language in the GLN contributes to the visibility of its speakers and the global popularity of the cultural content they produce."[38]

Supportive of the above findings are the words of noted linguist and author David Crystal, who wrote:

> Why a language becomes a global language has little to do with the number of people who speak it. It is much more to do with who those speakers are. Latin became an international language throughout the Roman Empire, but this was not because the Romans were more numerous than the peoples they subjugated. They were simply more powerful.[39]

Additional evidence of the international adoption of English lies in the world's universities. Some selective universities in South Korea have recently instituted English-only instruction in their curriculums.[40] This is not necessarily prudent given the added anxiety and loss of higher order vocabulary likely more accessible in the speakers' native Korean. English as a medium of instruction (EMI) in China, especially at younger ages, has come under a great deal of criticism. Although China has made learning English a priority for their future competitiveness, the quality of bilingual instruction in China has been marginal, perhaps due to the pace of expectations and the enormous scale of the task. According to *The Economist*, "Just over [one million] English-language staff teach over [200 million] Chinese pupils."[41]

Europe's non-native English-speaking countries have not been immune to the EMI trend at the university level. James Coleman of the UK's Open University contends this is at least partly due to an oversupply of universities below the elite level, competition for international students, and the marketization of higher education (e.g., branding of schools and referring to students as customers). Higher education, as an industry, has gravitated toward English to give its institutions relevance and access to global consumers.[42] Still, there are some universities that resist the urge of Englishization, including South Africa's Stellenbosch University. Steeped in apartheid roots, many students and professors there want English to become the main instructional language. Stellenbosch's university council has resisted, preferring a dual language campus of English and Afrikaans.[43]

Lots of Different Englishes

I recall a scene in the postapocalyptic film *Mad Max Beyond Thunderdome*. Max (played by Mel Gibson) stumbles upon a batch of feral children living in the wilderness. They speak a variant of Australian English Slang that is fractured with metaphors and symbology. Perhaps not the raw material of great English poetry, it is easily discernible nonetheless with its own rules, mythology, and character.

Global language dominance today does not guarantee a leadership position tomorrow. Yet Latin, for example, still lives in many forms, be it as a root word, a *Harry Potter* spell, legal jargon, or catchphrase printed on currency.

Again, dynamism and adaptability are vital for a strong language. In *The Language Wars*, Henry Hitchings writes, "English is taking on more and more local colour in the different places where it is used. Accordingly, where the number of languages in the world is diminishing, the number of Englishes is increasing."[44]
Roger that. Out.

Contra Maxims for English

English is the dominant global language. Cross-cultural knowledge matters more than mastery of multiple tongues. Learn a language because you want to. Instead of a second language, become proficient in mathematics, computer programming, or quantitative literacy. Learn to code, in English.

Notes

1. Yoko Masuda, "The Race to Beef Up Japan's Coast Guard," *The Wall Street Journal's Japan Real Time*, 27 Oct 2012, http://blogs.wsj.com /japanrealtime/2012/10/27/the-race-to-beef-up-japans-coast-guard / (accessed Feb 23, 2015).

2. David Crystal, *English as a Global Language* (Cambridge, UK: Cambridge University Press, 2003), 69.

3. EF Education First, *English Proficiency Index for Companies*, 2014, http://www.ef.com/__/~/media/centralefcom/epi/v4/downloads /epi-c/ef-epi-c-english-191114.pdf. Note: Survey conducted in 2013 involved over 105,000 employees from 31 countries.

4. Jacques Melitz, "English as a Global Language," SIRE Discussion Paper, SIRE-DP-2015-61, Scottish Institute for Research in Economics, 2015, http://repo.sire.ac.uk/bitstream/handle/10943/656 /SIRE_DP_2015_61.pdf?sequence=1

5. Jeffrey Jones, "Most in the U.S. Say it's Essential that Immigrants Learn English," Gallup, 9 Aug 2013, http://www.gallup.com/poll /163895/say-essential-immigrants-learn-english.aspx

6. John McMillian, "Against Foreign Language Requirements," *The American Historian*, Aug 2014, http://tah.oah.org/august-2014 /against-language-requirements/ (accessed Feb 10, 2016).

7. Swaan, Abram de, *Words of the World: The Global Language System* (Cambridge, United Kingdom: Polity Press, 2001); James Coleman, "English-medium Teaching in European Higher Education," *Language Teaching* 39, no. 1 (2006): 1–14; M. Paul Lewis, Gary F. Simons and Charles D. Fennig (Eds.) *Ethnologue: Languages of the World, 18th ed.* (Dallas, Texas: SIL International. 2015). Online version: http://www .ethnologue.com. (accessed Feb 16, 2016). Note: de Swaan (2001) and Coleman (2006) world language estimates number roughly 6,000; Lewis et al. (2015) peg global languages at 7,102.

8. Robert McCrum, William Cran, and Robert MacNeil, *The Story of English* (New York, NY: Elisabeth Sifton Books–Viking, 1986).

9. *The Adventure of English: 500 A.D. to 2000 A.D.,* Films for the Humanities and Sciences, 2004, Eight-part series, (DVD), Part 1.

10. Ibid., Part 2.

11. Tyler Cowen, *Creative Destruction: How Globalization is Changing the World's Culture* (Princeton, NJ: Princeton University Press, 2002), 83.

12. Ibid.

13. Ibid.

14. *Knowledge at Wharton*, "Acting Legend Kamal Haasan Looks to the Future of Indian Movies," 31 Mar 2016, http://knowledge .wharton.upenn.edu/article/acting-legend-kamal-haasan-looks-to -the-future-of-indian-movies/?utm_source=kw_newsletter&utm _medium=email&utm_campaign=2016-03-31 (accessed Apr 7, 2016).

15. *The Economist*, "The Mute Leading the Mute," 14 Feb 2015, 54

16. EF Education First, *English Proficiency Index for Companies*.

17. Anne Kankaanranta and Leena Louhiala-Salmimen, "What Language Does Global Business Speak? – The Concept and Development of BELF," *Iberica* 26, no. 26 (2013): 17–34.

18. Pamela Rogerson-Revell, "Participation and Performance in International Business Meetings," *English for Specific Purposes* 27, no. 3 (2008): 338–360.

19. Tsedal Neeley, "Global Business Speaks English: Why You Need a Language Strategy Now," *Harvard Business Review* 90, no. 5 (May 2012): 116–124.

20. Tsedal Neeley, "Language Matters: Status Loss and Achieved Status Distinctions in Global Organizations," *Organization Science* 24, no. 20 (2013): 476.

21. Neeley, "Global Business Speaks English"

22. Martine Haas and Jonathan Cummings, "Barriers to Knowledge Seeking within MNC Teams: Which Differences Matter Most?" *Journal of International Business Studies* 46, no. 1 (2015): 36–62.

23. Susanne Ehrenreich, "English as a Business Lingua Franca in a German Multinational Corporation," *Journal of Business Communication* 47, no. 4 (2010): 408.

24. Pamela Hinds, Tsedal Neeley, and Catherine Durnell Crampton, "Language as a Lightning Rod: Power Contests, Emotion Regulation, and Subgroup Dynamics in Global Teams," *Journal of International Business Studies* 45, no. 5 (2014): 540.

25. Ibid., 556.

26. EF Education First, *English Proficiency Index for Companies.*

27. Leena Louhiala-Salminen, Mirjaliisa Charles, and Anne Kankaanranta, "English as a Lingua Franca in Nordic Corporate Mergers: Two Case Companies," *English for Specific Purposes* 24, no. 4 (2005): 402.

28. Ibid.

29. Ibid., 417.

30. Ibid., 419.

31. Bill Fisher, "Why English, Not Mandarin, is the Language of Innovation," *Harvard Business Review*, 12 Jan 2015, Digital Edition, https://hbr.org/2015/01/why-english-not-mandarin-is-the-language-of-innovation (accessed Feb 4, 2016).

32. W3 Techs Web Technology Surveys, "Usage of Content for Websites," http://w3techs.com/technologies/overview/content_language/all (accessed Feb 8, 2016). Note: Methodology includes a sample of ten million most popular websites; subdomains and re-directs are excluded. Rankings are tabulated daily.

33. Kyle Chayka, "Developers Teach Apple Chinese," *Bloomberg Businessweek*, 10–23 Aug 2015, 36, 38.

34. *The Economist*, "The Translation Industry: Say What?" 7 Feb 2015, 62.

35. Michael Luca, Jon Kleinberg, and Sendhil Mullainathan, "Algorithms Need Managers, too," *Harvard Business Review*, Jan–Feb 2016, 99.

36. Gideon Lewis-Kraus, "Google and Other Tech Dreamers Think Machines Can Make Languages Superfluous," *New York Times Magazine*, 7 Jun 2015, 52.

37. Shahar Ronen, Bruno Goncalves, Kevin Hu, Alessandro Vespignani, Steven Pinker, and Cesar Hidalgo, "Links that Speak: The Global Language Network and its Association with Global Fame," *Proceedings of the National Academy of Sciences of the United States of America*, 2014, http://www.pnas.org/content/111/52/E5616.full.pdf Note: book translation tables were retrieved on Feb 4, 2016 from http://language.media.mit.edu/rankings/books

38. Ibid., 1.

39. David Crystal, *English as a Global Language* (Cambridge, UK: Cambridge University Press, 2003), 7.

40. Hyun-Sook Kang, "English-only Instruction at Korean Universities: Help or Hindrance to Higher Learning?" *English Today* 28, no. 1 (2012): 29–34.

41. *The Economist*, "The Mute Leading the Mute," 54

42. James Coleman, "English-medium Teaching in European Higher Education," *Language Teaching* 39, no. 1 (2006): 1–14.

43. *The Economist*, "The Ivory Tower is too White," 5 Dec 2015, 49.

44. Henry Hitchings, *The Language Wars: A History of Proper English* (New York, NY: Farrar, Straus and Giroux, 2011), 309.

CHAPTER 3

Introverts Cannot Lead Effectively

It's not that I'm so smart, it's just that I stay with problems longer.
—Albert Einstein

Your vision will become clear only when you look into your heart. Who looks outside, dreams; who looks inside, awakens.
—Carl Gustav Jung

Introverts have gained some overdue respect of late due to the economic success of bashful tech entrepreneurs and the release of recent books uncovering the virtues of introversion. The rise of nouveau geek chic can also be linked to successful pop culture phenomena such as television's *Big Bang Theory*. But by and large, introverts have been much maligned over the years, especially since the dawning of the industrial revolution. Imagine a younger, more rural America with just over 15 percent of the population living in cities in 1850.[1] Homespun values of self-sufficiency, hard work, character, modesty, morality, and religious adherence were prevalent. Yet as the nation urbanized and lurched into the late 19th and early 20th centuries, dramatic sociocultural and technological shifts occurred.

A boom in capitalism and its requisite means of production spawned the need for sales people to goose demand. Look no further for an example of the transformative selling class than Dale Carnegie, himself a quiet farm boy in his youth. Inspired by a traveling orator as a kid, the charismatic artistry that built a self-help and corporate training empire was slow in coming. Carnegie worked tirelessly to perfect his craft and business formula. In short, he trained relentlessly to suppress his natural introversion to become an icon of outward positivity.[2]

Extroverted leading roles in motion pictures have been celebrated more than their humble counterparts. Think of the diabolical charm of Burt Lancaster in the film adaption of Sinclair Lewis' *Elmer Gantry*, the playful hucksterism of Robert Preston as *The Music Man*, and the megalomania of Orson Welles in *Citizen Kane*. All three portrayals are emblematic of the lure of charisma and extroversion. Firebrands that get others excited by being excited. But Hollywood hasn't ignored the virtues of introversion. The big screen has given us stalwart introverts such as Gregory Peck's Atticus Finch in *To Kill a Mockingbird*, and Tom Hanks as Captain Miller in *Saving Private Ryan*.

Yet our societal default is unquestionably extroversion. In a culture with a bias toward outgoingness, you hear introverts described as shy, quiet, timid, pensive, socially awkward, antisocial, loners, wallflowers, reticent, mild-mannered, and lacking confidence. Unfairly, descriptors for introverts are often negative, as if it is a character flaw or pathological delinquency. The enlightened among us know better, of course.

It is important to note that introversion is not synonymous with shyness. Both introverts and extroverts can be shy. In *The Introvert's Advantage*, author and psychoanalyst Marti Olsen Laney describes shyness as "social anxiety, an extreme self-consciousness when one is around people." She further explains shyness as being "not who *you are* (like introversion), it is what you think *other* people think you are."[3]

In contrast, Laney describes introversion as a ". . . healthy capacity to tune into your inner world. . . a constructive and creative quality that is found in many independent thinkers. . ." She adds, "Introverts have social skills, they like people, and they enjoy some types of socializing."[4] One team of scholars described introverts, relative to extroverts, as "more quiet and reserved, more socially aloof, and less interpersonally effective."[5]

The positive qualities of introversion are often overlooked. The dichotomy of *waiting to speak* versus *thinking out loud* can be to an introvert's advantage. The introvert may use the extra time to produce a more thoughtful response or solution. Introverts are less likely to say something really dumb or inappropriate because of the built-in delay they possess. It's as if they have their own little network censor residing in their subconscious.

The introverted leader has a more reflective style, prefers one-on-one conversations, tends to think more deeply about issues, and is more comfortable when focusing on fewer things at one time. Extroverted leaders have a broader capacity, but they don't often drill down into the nitty gritty details. Overall, however, there is no discernible difference in IQ scores among introverts and extroverts.

If you're an introvert working with or for competent professionals who know the value of other smart people (that just happen to be quiet), you are in luck. Over time, colleagues should notice that talented introverts offer valuable insights and contributions. Leaders that are aware of introverts in their charge can use their talents effectively. However, there are many in the workplace that view outwardly expressed confidence as more valuable than less demonstrative demeanors.

We are a society hung up on quick responses, eye candy, and slick packaging. We care too much for *how* and *by whom* information is delivered and not enough for *what* the information means. Too often we are led by style instead of substance. Here lies another constant management conundrum: knowing the difference between hasty, superfluous commentary and contemplative, valuable input. The fault in the maxim *Introverts cannot lead effectively* is as much a failing of followership as it is leadership. Blame is seldom aimed at the group or the obedient masses. Nevertheless, the introverted leader must work to overcome the shallow and mistaken assumptions of the collective.

The good news, if you are an introvert, is that there is nothing wrong with you. Additionally, you are not alone. The numbers vary, but anywhere from one-third to one-half of the population are considered introverted. Jennifer Kanhweiler, author of *The Introverted Leader*, estimates that 40 percent of executives are introverts.[6]

Looking at self-reported personality preferences of over 23,000 general or operations managers, published by CPP, Inc., 39.5 percent were scored as introverts. Professions exhibiting higher percentages of introverts to extroverts include microbiologist (57 percent), computer hardware engineer (57.1 percent), and actuary (58.1 percent). Job titles with introverts representing less than half of the sample included sales managers at 23.1 percent, marketing managers at 30.9 percent, and management analysts with 43 percent.[7] Importantly, these numbers are descriptive and do not involve any performance aspects of the individuals in the samples.

Introvert as a descriptor gained prominence in the early 1920s due to the work of psychoanalyst Carl Jung. It seems fitting that an extrovert-introvert (E-I) spectrum was devised during the extrovert wave of the roaring 20s. The Myers-Briggs Type Indicator (MBTI®) is based on Jung's early studies, and is used by 89 percent of Fortune 100 firms as a tool for assessing traits of employees and job candidates.[8] The MBTI utilizes four scaled dimensions, with the E-I measure considered the most valid.[9] The other three scales are sensation-intuition, thinking-feeling, and judging-perceiving. There are 16 possible permutations of indicators using the MBTI framework.

The terms *preferences* and *indicators* are purposeful. CPP, Inc. emphasizes that the MBTI survey is not a *test* of personality, but merely a gauge for the individual's preferences within the four dimensions.

No discussion of personality traits should ignore the psychology discipline's so-called Big Five personality factors, including extraversion (which by extension includes introversion); conscientiousness; agreeableness; neuroticism (also called low emotional stability); and openness to new experiences. Researchers testing for personality traits often combine the MBTI with the Big Five dimensions to help explain their models and results. Table 3.1 contains a brief summary of characteristics associated with introverts and extroverts:

Table 3.1 Traits for introverts and extroverts[10]

Introvert Traits	Extrovert Traits
Energized by solitude, quiet	Energized by being around lots of people
Inward focus; good at resisting distraction	External focus
Internal rewards provide confidence; often reluctant to receive external praise	External rewards are important, welcomed
Focus is in-depth, on just one or a few issues at a time	Broad, topical approach to issues
Prefers one-on-one conversation	Likes to communicate and meet in groups
Multitasking may cause stress	More accomplished at multitasking
Delayed, more thoughtful responses	Often thinks out loud, offers quick answers
Reserved, quiet, reflective	Enthusiastic, gregarious, spontaneous
Prefer writing, and e-mails	Prefer speaking, texting, and instant messaging
Performs well in online collaborations	More suited for in-person brainstorming sessions

Susan Cain, author of the popular book *Quiet: the Power of Introverts in a World that Can't Stop Talking*, has done much to dispel some of the taboos associated with introversion. More importantly, she has raised the alarm concerning trends that may inadvertently marginalize introverts in both education and work settings. Cain labels one dark force as the *New Groupthink*. For example, she visited a fourth grade classroom and noticed a sign that listed rules for working in small groups. One chilling edict prescribed, "You can't ask a teacher for help unless everyone in your group has the same question."[11] Yikes! Rules like this give socialism a bad name (and deservedly so). Lil' group thinkers today, masters of conformity tomorrow! This is obviously not an ideal learning environment for young introverts.

Cain also laments the open floorplans of today's workspaces. Well intentioned, these open spaces are meant to foster group collaboration, communication, and creativity.[12] Formerly, walls and cozy office confines represented structure and orderly compartmentalization for many introverts. A closed door provided safe harbor from unwanted interruptions. Contrastingly, many workspaces promote an office culture with a zealous open door policy. How is an introvert supposed to thrive in such a free-ranging workplace where much of the job feels like awkwardly attending a mandatory office party? For many introverts, this is akin to a conspiracy against solitude and individual creativity.

Let's recall the introvert's preference for some me-time and more intimate settings. Due to the rise in background noise from open office plans, architect Chu Foxlin recently proposed isolation cones made of felt that could hang from the ceiling. I am not joking. Thankfully, there is at least some push back against the antiprivacy movement. I'm all for open common space at work because it's where a lot of informal yet valuable idea exchange takes place. But I think the pendulum has swung too far. Writing for *The Atlantic*, Olga Khazan summed this up nicely when she snarked, "Even for the most gregarious of workers, it seems, sometimes hell is a communal workbench shared with other people."[13]

Regarding career advancement and leadership positions, introverts are at a distinct disadvantage in the exposed atmosphere just described. If the environment does not enable the talents of the introverted, how can they truly perform, contribute, shine, develop, and get promoted?

If the physical space and culture of an organization is biased against the strengths of introverts, the results are lost productivity and disadvantaged work climates for the more pensive among us. Indeed, *The Economist* recently spoke of this environment by admonishing, "Most companies worry about discriminating against their employees on the basis of race, gender or sexual preference. But they give little thought to their shabby treatment of introverts."[14]

While the labels for introverts and extroverts provide a clean delineation to describe people, there is a growing awareness of a third category: the *ambivert*. Ambiverts live in both worlds and tend to score in the middle range of the E-I spectrum. At times they are extremely social beings but also spend lots of time working, thinking, and reflecting alone.

Another term used for the multitude of tweeners on the E-I continuum is *centrovert*. Centroverts are said to have the capacity to "mediate, negotiate, and collaborate simply because they have an inherent understanding of different styles."[15]

For the record, I have identified myself as an ambivert based on multiple MBTI self-assessments, although I often score as a marginal introvert. Furthermore, I'm an ambivert with wild swings to both poles of the continuum. Some days I crave social contact and a party, other times I relish being the only person left in my entire building at work. Research by Adam Grant of the Wharton School claims approximately two-thirds of us are ambiverts, with the balance being strong introverts or strong extroverts.[16]

In 2013 Grant published a study of 340 outbound-call-center representatives that found higher revenue associated with ambiverts. Findings revealed a curvilinear relationship indicating a diminishing return with revenue as a representative's degree of extraversion increased. Grant reflected in the paper's notes that ambiverts may "devote greater time to listening without facing the risk of understimulation."[17]

Notable Type "I"s

Many renowned business leaders have been described as introverts, including Microsoft founder Bill Gates, investment sage and Berkshire Hathaway CEO Warren Buffett, and Apple CEO Tim Cook. Gates and Buffett prefer more intimate surroundings, but their professional obligations require them to be the face of their respective organizations.

The on-stage version of Tim Cook is a good example of an introvert acting outside of his innate temperament. Cook leads the most valuable company in the world very publically out of necessity, but with a confidence unaccompanied by the personal bravado of his predecessor, Steve Jobs.

Famous political leaders that are viewed predominately as introverts include Abraham Lincoln, Mahatma Gandhi, and Eleanor Roosevelt. Lincoln's prowess lay in his writing, profound deep thinking, and understanding of others' motivations. Recall Gandhi's contemplative, nonconfrontational style and passive resistance. Gandhi preferred to build trust and slowly win people over to his ways, being less divisive, and resisting snap judgments. Eleanor Roosevelt was shy and preferred listening to talking, but was still courageous and productive. She led numerous groups and political initiatives. Her resignation from the Daughters of the American Revolution, because they refused to let an African American woman sing the national anthem, was a bold and necessary act of leadership.[18]

Frances Perkins, President Franklin D. Roosevelt's Secretary of Labor (1933–1945) and the first female cabinet member in the United States, was media averse and reluctant to hear new information. *New York Times* columnist and author David Brooks, who considers Perkins a personal hero, opined that her reticence and lack of engagement with the media was detrimental to her work.[19] While Perkins' introverted constitution may have at times worked against her, one could argue that without her deep thinking and reflective side she may have been ineffectual at getting American Labor behind the New Deal.

Apple cofounder Steve Wozniak, credited by many (including himself) as the creator of the personal computer (PC), is most definitely an introvert. In his enjoyable autobiography *iWoz*, Wozniak describes his early forays in 1975 with the Homebrew Club, an informal group of computer and electronics enthusiasts. Wozniak would bring his wares and schematics to Homebrew meetings, held in the garage of a Menlo Park club member, and just wait for people to ask him questions. He was too afraid to speak first. Wozniak recounts:

> I was never the kind of person who had the courage to raise his hand during the Homebrew main meeting and say, "Hey, look at this great computer advance I've made." No, I could never have said that in front of a whole garageful of people.[20]

Wozniak cheerfully recalls his construction of the Apple I. After a normal shift at Hewlett-Packard (H-P) (working on calculators) and a quick dinner, he would return to the solitude of his H-P cubicle and assemble what would be the world's first PC. He liked working there late into the night "because it was an engineering kind of environment." It was there that Wozniak became the first person to make characters appear on a video screen in real time while typing them. While there were lots of value-added group encounters along the way, Wozniak did the bulk of his thinking, designing, building, and troubleshooting *alone*.[21]

Former Boston Consulting Group chief executive John Clarkeson was the antithesis of his predecessor and most of the partners in the firm. Although the management consulting industry is teeming with aggressive extroverts, Clarkeson thrived while being described as "quiet, self-effacing, a declared believer in the power of empathy and of listening instead of talking." After serving 12 years as CEO he was Chairman for another 9 years.[22]

A few more accomplished introverts that have been leaders in their respective fields include the great inventor Thomas Edison, six-time NBA champion Michael Jordan, Super Bowl winning coaches Bill Belichick and Tony Dungy, and award winning film makers Steven Spielberg, Clint Eastwood and Alfred Hitchcock.

Leaving the Comfort Zone

Paul Maritz, former president and CEO of cloud software giant VMware, acknowledges that he is an introvert. In an interview with *The New York Times*, Maritz candidly revealed:

> It's my nature to be an introvert. And being a leader, you can't just be an introvert. People want to know that they can emotionally connect with you – that you're, in some deep way, going on a journey with them and that you recognize them. And that requires you to open up to people and reach out to them and connect with them. Left to myself, I will retreat into my office, so I have to be aware of that.[23]

Not simply a fake-it-till-you-make-it transformation process, introverted leaders often have to work on their *outside game* to be effective mentors and motivators. Cambridge University psychology professor Brian Little claims, "Many of us, as a result of our vocational or professional demands, act out of character." Professor Little sees the ability to perform at both ends of the E-I spectrum as a valuable skill.[24] Indeed, nearly 100 years ago Carl Jung viewed our adaptability to be contingent upon how well we could traverse the E-I continuum.[25] Effective managers and leaders benefit from solid interpersonal skills, be it articulating goals, displaying empathy, or relating well with others.

Author Laura Vanderkam, most known for her books on time management, faced her demons when success forced her to transition from writing books in solitude to speaking about them in public. Her story is quite typical given that introverts would rather write than talk, and are more eloquent with the written word versus the spoken. Her solution was to prepare for talks by getting to know a handful of audience members beforehand, and to practice. This preparation, including some selective memorization for confidence-building, helped Vanderkam make the extroverted experience of public speaking feel more natural, comfortable, and even enjoyable. Not completely stress free mind you, but much more tolerable.[26]

A big issue with introverts in their careers is invisibility. Professionals trying to work their way up a career ladder or corporate pecking order need visibility. It's important that your talents and accomplishments are recognized by the right people. Introverts are often at a disadvantage in this regard as they are less likely to be tooting their own horn. Perhaps you have witnessed extroverted colleagues getting lots of notice, plum assignments, and maybe quicker promotions. Some of those accolades may not be truly deserved, but people in power know their names, faces, and somehow connect them to achievements and competencies. This is by no means an indictment of extroverts, but there are more than a few folks out there that, without their charismatic charms and social prowess, wouldn't last a day in a truly meritocratic organization.

So, the introvert needs to prepare, practice, and get visible.[27] It may be stressful at times, but it will pay off. *The Wall Street Journal's* Joann Lublin has written about executives overcoming introverted instincts to help not only their careers but also the performance of their employees and firms. Lublin points to introvert success stories including Google's cofounder and CEO Larry Page, Colgate-Palmolive's chief executive Ian Cook, and Campbell Soup's head honcho Douglas Conant. These leaders are able to call on coping mechanisms to lessen the shortcomings of introversion without losing the benefits. Remember, many introverts have the ability to hone in and focus during individualized conversations, and also listen better than most extroverts.[28] They can train intensively to acquire an extrovert skill set.

Lublin also remarked about negative stereotypes besetting introverts. She cites a survey from the job website TheLadders.com that reported 65 percent of senior managers felt introversion was a career obstacle.[29] This same study indicated only 6 percent of over 1,500 managers surveyed believed introverts made better CEOs than nonintroverts, while 47 percent felt extroverts were better, and 47 percent claimed there was no difference.[30] Again, it may not be fair, but these perceptions linger. Introverts need to overcome these biases.

Who Says Extroverts are Better Leaders?

There is certainly no shortage of scholarly research in the domain that combines leadership and personality. However, it is difficult to study high-level leaders (e.g., corporate CEOs, senior government officials) given their time constraints and poor compliance as survey respondents. Nevertheless, there are some useful findings that help inform our examination of introversion and extroversion as leadership performance indicators. It is important to note that leadership styles and personal characteristics have not been reliable predictors of organizational performance. Numerous studies have yielded mixed results.[31]

While introverted leaders are often maligned for seeming too distant, mysteriously quiet, or not as capable as extroverts, extroverted leaders are far from ideal. One particular problem is that a leader's personality may overshadow the interests of the firm. Jim Collins, author of *Good to Great*, warned that firms with outsized, big personality CEOs ran the risk of mediocre organizational performance. Collins' research noted that "less charismatic leaders often produce better long-term results than their more charismatic counterparts."[32] Rewind about 2,500 years and you find a similar spirit in the words of an ancient Chinese philosopher and founder of Taoism. Lao Tzu once said (probably in a hushed tone), "A leader is best when people barely know he exists, when his work is done, his aim fulfilled, they will say: we did it ourselves."

In a study of 128 CEOs of major U.S. corporations, organizational performance was positively correlated with subsequent perceptions of leader charisma, but attitudes of CEO charisma were not correlated with subsequent organizational performance. Charisma in this study was scored from senior management impressions of their own CEO's level of charisma.[33] Incidentally, asking corporate senior management to rate their boss's personality, even with assurances of confidentiality, is a problematic proposition at best—especially given the small sample from each firm.

In a study of pizza shop bosses and subordinates, the performance of groups headed by extroverted leaders differed depending on the nature of the subordinates. Higher profits were attained by passive groups led by extroverts, but extroverted leaders were not as successful with proactive groups of employees. Findings also suggested that introverted leaders listen better, are receptive to employee ideas, and are proactive in improving work methods. Similar results from this field study were duplicated in a laboratory setting. These studies pointed out that extraverted leadership can be detrimental to group performance in addition to being beneficial under certain circumstances.[34] For instance, there is evidence that extroverts may be better suited for situations requiring a transformational leadership role.[35]

A study published in the *British Journal of Management* tested for personality traits of 900 people across multiple industries to see what characteristics were linked to managerial levels. The research utilized MBTI and the Big Five frameworks. Findings showed conscientiousness, extraversion, and MBTI intuition were positively related to managerial level. It also reported neuroticism, MBTI introversion, and sensing were negatively correlated with the level of management position. A closer look at the results, however, reveals extremely weak relatedness strength for all the correlations—be they statistically significant or not. Now those are the results, but the researchers' interpretation of the findings is confounding.

The researchers claimed that their results "attest to the utility of personality tests used within the occupational community, for selection and assessment of suitability for promotion to senior managerial roles."[36] I beg to differ with this conclusion. The results, had there been more robust relationships found, would only have reinforced status quo opinions and shadow effects of certain traits (i.e., introversion and neuroticism do not complement leadership ability).

Interestingly, a recent study in the *Academy of Management Journal* found that, over time, "Extraversion was correlated with status losses and disappointing expectations for contributions to group tasks." Furthermore, neuroticism was shown to have status gains over the same time period, likely due to surpassing the initial expectations of respondents.[37] Bear in mind that neuroticism is very different from the E-I spectrum as a personality construct, yet similarly maligned. Group members apparently made judgments based on their preconceived notion of traits and how they would translate to subsequent performance. This study showed how actual group behavior and experience reversed opinions on the status of fellow group members. The study authors, from The University of California, Los Angeles (UCLA) and Rutgers, playfully referred to their findings as "the dark side of extraversion and the bright side of neuroticism." Good for them!

Leadership research is similar to investigations that study entrepreneurs. Scholars try to identify what the common traits of successful leaders and entrepreneurs are, as if they could then bottle these traits and sell them. It is hard to isolate predictive traits as causes of superior performance, however, as some of the aforementioned research findings have indicated. Aileen Lee, founder and partner of venture capital firm Cowboy Ventures, struggles with sizing up entrepreneurs for potential investments. When asked what she looks for in company founders, she thoughtfully shares:

There's not a formula. I've learned that you really cannot judge a book by its cover. You have to get under the hood and spend some quality time with someone to understand what they're really good at. If you don't, then you're only going to back extrovert, Type A people who are really good at selling. And it's not clear that that's a requirement for building a great company. You could be a creative genius or a product genius, or you might have an insight into a market that is really special but you're not that good at explaining it.[38]

Countless leadership books have highlighted skills such as listening, empathy, deliberation, and thoughtful communication (e.g., one-on-one dialogue) as beneficial leadership qualities. These are also qualities possessed by many introverts. Organizations are missing out on extraordinarily talented individuals when they look myopically and sometimes exclusively for more traditional leadership qualities such as charisma and outgoingness.

Contra Maxims for Introverted Leadership

Style points count, but substance matters more for leadership excellence. Introverts can lead effectively, especially with a sprinkling of acquired extraversion. Lastly, let's include an old standard that introverted leaders should learn to employ now and again: Toot your own horn!

Notes

1. United States Census, "Archives, Table 4. Population: 1790–1990," http://www.census.gov/population/www/cesusdata/files/table-4.pdf (accessed Aug 12, 2015). Note: U.S. population in 1900 was 39.6% urban, and 60.4% rural; the 2010 U.S. Census reported the urban population at over 80%.
2. Susan Cain, *Quiet: The Power of Introverts in a World that Can't Stop Talking* (New York, NY: Crown, 2012).
3. Marti Olsen Laney, *The Introvert Advantage: How to Thrive in an Extrovert World* (New York, NY: Workman Publishing, 2002), 43.
4. Ibid.
5. David Watson and Lee Clark, "Extraversion and its Positive Emotional Core," In R. Hogan, J. Johnson & S. Briggs (Eds.) *Handbook of Personality Psychology,* (San Diego, CA: Academic Press, 1997), 767.
6. Jennifer Kahnweiler, *The Introverted Leader* (San Francisco, CA: Berrett-Koehler, 2009), 1.

7. Nancy Schaubhut and Richard Thompson, *MBTI Type Tables for Occupations* (Mountain View, CA: CPP, Inc., 2012).

8. CPP, Inc., "Myers-Briggs Type Indicator," 2015, https://www.cpp.com/products/mbti/index.aspx (accessed Aug 1, 2015). Note: Myers-Briggs and MBTI are registered trademarks of The Myers-Briggs Foundation.

9. Laney, *The Introvert Advantage*

10. Note: Traits in Table 3.1 were sourced, in part, from Laney (2002), Kahnweiler (2009), CPP, Inc., and Laurie Helgo, "Revenge of the Introvert," *Psychology Today*, (Sep–Oct, 2010), 54–56.

11. Cain, *Quiet: The Power of Introverts*, 77

12. Ibid.

13. Olga Khazan, "Thinking Outside the Cube: How Offices Will Change – For Better and For Worse," *The Atlantic*, Sep 2015, 26.

14. *The Economist*, "Shhhh: Companies Would Benefit from Helping Introverts to Thrive," 10 Sep 2016, 59.

15. *Schott's Vocab: A Miscellany of Modern Words and Phrases*, "Centrovert," 20 Oct 2010, http://schott.blogs.nytimes.com/2010/10/20/20/centrovert/ (accessed Aug 6, 2015). Cited from a *TechRepublic* interview with Devora Zack, who introduced the term in her book *Networking for People Who Hate Networking*.

16. Elizabeth Bernstein, "Not Introvert, Nor Extrovert: The Adaptable Ambivert," *The Wall Street Journal*, 28 July 2015, D2.

17. Adam Grant, "Rethinking the Extraverted Sales Ideal: The Ambivert Advantage," *Psychological Science* 24, no. 6 (2013):1024–1030.

18. Cain, *Quiet: The Power of Introverts*

19. David Brooks, "Hilary's Big Test," *The New York Times*, 13 Mar 2015, A25.

20. Steve Wozniak and Gina Smith, *iWoz: How I Invented the Personal Computer, Co-founded Apple, and Had Fun Doing It* (New York, NY: W.W. Norton, 2006), 167.

21. Ibid.

22. Walter Keichel, *The Lords of Strategy: The Secret Intellectual History of the New Corporate World* (Boston, MA: Harvard Business Press, 2010), 266.

23. Adam Bryant, "Does Your Team Have the Four Essential Types?" *The New York Times,* 2 Oct 2010, http://www.nytimes.com/2010/10/03/business/03corner.html (accessed Aug 5, 2015).

24. Anna North, "Is Introversion Still a Liability in Politics?" *The New York Times,* 27 Feb 2015, http://op-talk.blogs.nytimes.com/2015/02/27/is-introversion-still-a-liability-in-politics/ (accessed Aug 10, 2015).

25. Laney, *The Introvert Advantage,* 28

26. Laura Vanderkam, "The Introvert on the Podium," *The New York Times,* 23 Nov 2014, BU10.

27. Kahnweiler, *The Introverted Leader*

28. Joann Lublin, "Introverted Execs Find Ways to Shine," *The Wall Street Journal,* 14 Apr 2011, http://www.wsj.com/articles/SB10001424052748703983104576263053775879800

29. Ibid.

30. Del Jones, "Not All CEOs are Extroverts," *USA Today,* 7 Jun 2006, http://usatoday30.usatoday.com/money/companies/management/2006-06-06-shy-ceo-usat_x.htm (accessed Aug 5, 2015).

31. Suzanne Carter and Charles Greer, "Strategic Leadership: Values, Styles, and Organizational Performance," *Journal of Leadership & Organizational Studies* 20, no. 4 (2013): 375–393.

32. Jim Collins, *Good to Great: Why Some Companies Make the Leap . . . and Others Don't* (New York, NY: Harper Business, 2001), 72.

33. Bradley Agle, Nandu Nagarajan, Jeffrey Sonnenfeld and Dhinu Srinivasan, "Does CEO Charisma Matter? An Empirical Analysis of the Relationship Among Organizational Performance, Environmental Uncertainty, and Top Management Team Perceptions of CEO Charisma," *Academy of Management Journal* 49, no. 1 (2006): 161–174.

34. Adam Grant, Francesca Gino and David Hofman, "Reversing the Extraverted Leadership Advantage: The Role of Employee Proactivity," *Academy of Management Journal* 54, no. 3 (2011):528–550.

35. Joyce Bono and Timothy Judge, "Personality and Transformational and Transactional Leadership: A Meta-analysis," *Journal of Applied Psychology* 89, no. 5 (2004): 901–910.

36. Jennifer Moutafi, Adrian Furnham and John Crump, "Is Managerial Level Related to Personality?" *British Journal of Management* 18, no. 3 (2007): 272–280.

37. Corinne Bendersky and Neha Parikh Shah, "The Downfall of Extraverts and Rise of Neurotics: The Dynamic Process of Status Allocation in Task Groups," *Academy of Management Journal* 56, no. 2 (2013): 387–406.

38. Adam Bryant, "Aim to See Beneath the Surface," *The New York Times*, 6 Dec 2015, BU2.

CHAPTER 4

Worrying is Counterproductive

Optimistic bias can be both a blessing and a risk, you should be both happy and wary if you are temperamentally optimistic.
—Daniel Kahneman, *Thinking, Fast and Slow*

Fear of competition, fear of bankruptcy, fear of being wrong and fear of losing can all be powerful motivators.
—Andy Grove, *Only the Paranoid Survive*

You may recall the hit song "Don't Worry Be Happy" by Bobby McFerrin. The song implied that worrying made no sense and only led to more personal stress. Whatever it is that worries you, relax, it will pass soon enough.

McFerrin was right about the passing part. Nearly everything that stresses us is temporary to some extent, including that report your boss wants by 5:00 p.m.; your new product forecast that cascades a beehive of other decisions; a time-sensitive decision on maintenance contracts for the truck fleet; and even that job offer you're fretting has a perishable shelf life. Worries will often go away if you let them. Some will come back to bite you later on regardless of whether you worried yourself sick over them or not. Nowadays, you're likely to hear the common idiom *no worries* tossed about as a casual reminder to fret less and stay loose.

Warnings about the ills of worrying run deep in American culture. Dale Carnegie's mid-20th-century best seller *How to Stop Worrying and Start Living* was a less than cryptic prescription for those dogged by stress and anxiety. Carnegie was uncompromising in his demonization of all things worrisome. Chapters in his book include "How to Break the

Worry Habit Before it Breaks You" and "How to Crowd Worry Out of Your Mind." An essay by boxing legend Jack Dempsey, included as part of a compilation of famous people and their woes in Carnegie's book, spoke of worry as the champ's greatest opponent.[1] Alternatively, I suggest that it was worry that kept Dempsey's guard up and contributed to his success in the ring.

Francis O'Gorman, in his 2015 book *Worrying: A Literary and Cultural History*, describes the origins and cultural meanings of worry. While the concept of worry has benefited the species since the cave dwelling days, the *word* worry doesn't appear in early, authorized Bibles such as the King James Version. Worry was inserted in modern, more liberally translated Bible editions (e.g., *Good News Translation* and the *New King James Version*) as a way to appease readers finding traditional Bible prose too cumbersome.[2]

Early definitions of worry included *choke, strangle*, and *bite*.[3] Indeed, it was this violent connotation that Queen Margaret recites in Shakespeare's *Richard III*, "That dog, that had his teeth before his eyes, to worry lambs and lap their gentle blood."[4] Shakespeare only used worry (or a variation of it) four times in all his works. The Bard preferred his characters to *fret*, and more often than not, to *fear*.[5] It wasn't until the mid-19th century when the meaning of worry blended into the more solicitous concepts of fear and apprehension that we are familiar with today.[6]

O'Gorman frames worry as a *"set of questions* about the future that generate imagined chains of *cause-and-effect*. Worry deals with what's *plausible* to the worrier and, in this sense, is a *form of logic* working inside set premises."[7] O'Gorman also refers to worry as weedlike and "circular," leading one to conclude of worry as a psychological manifestation not easily dissuaded.

The rapid growth of globalization and improved standard of living have ironically increased our everyday worries. O'Gorman points out that "Worry is only possible in a world of choice."[8] He connects choice to our growing disbelief of predestination by saying:

> Worry flourishes where human beings believe they can decide outcomes for themselves from a reasoned assessment of what the options might be; an assessment, perhaps, which tries to take

everything into account. Worry flourishes even more when we think that there is a right decision to be made about the future and we have to use our powers to discern it rather than rely on divine authority.[9]

Generally speaking, modernity bemoans worry as a net negative. Despite its mendacity, the maxim *Worrying is counterproductive* has accrued a gloomy yet resilient cultural currency over the last two centuries. Brooders, realists, and devil's advocates have been admonished with "You'll worry yourself to death," and labeled as worry warts. I contest this popular view and believe that worry has been undeservingly maligned. When not overdone, worrying provides a wealth of cognitive and preparatory benefits in complex situations where decisions are compulsory.

Next, I'll cover some commonly misapplied terminology and provide a brief review of relevant research, which I hope leads you to challenge the dubious claim that *Worrying is counterproductive*. I'll then provide some practical accounts of worrying's dividends including its value in strategic planning.

Coming to Terms with Worry

For clarity it is necessary to delineate worry and a few related terms that are used interchangeably even though they are technically very different. The American Psychiatric Association refers to worry as *apprehensive expectation*.[10] Academic psychologists define worry as a primarily cognitive activity, a "type of thinking related to the future and to future's uncertain outcomes."[11] "Worry involves thinking about personally relevant and potentially negative future events."[12] Furthermore, worry often "resembles problem solving" and reduces the chances of "surprise even when an anticipated threat does in fact materialize."[13]

Closely associated with worry is *anxiety*, which is "the apprehensive anticipation of future danger or misfortune accompanied by a feeling of worry, distress, and/or somatic symptoms of tension."[14] Worry is the "primary diagnostic criterion" of anxiety.[15] Broadly speaking (since there is no universal agreement on a clear distinction between anxiety and worry), nonpathological anxiety is like a ramped up form of worry. Anxiety is more unrealistic, imaginative, and physiological than worry. Anxiety invokes "lingering apprehension, or a sense of worry or tension, the sources of which may be totally unclear."[16]

As we increase the level of anxiety, we may begin to see physical symptoms of stress, such as sweating, visible nervousness, and elevated heart rate. General anxiety disorder (GAD) is a more serious and potentially debilitating condition. According to the American Psychological Association, GAD involves worries that are "excessive and typically interfere significantly with psychosocial functioning, whereas the worries of everyday life are not excessive and are perceived as more manageable and may be put off when more pressing matters arise." Additionally, worries with GAD are more "pervasive, pronounced, and distressing" and remain problematic for at least 6 months.[17]

Another worry-related term used liberally and with regularity is *fear*. Fear is more accurately described as "the emotional response to real or perceived imminent threat, whereas anxiety is anticipation of future threat." Fear is commonly associated with "surges of autonomic arousal necessary for fight or flight, thoughts of immediate danger."[18]

Two more closely aligned terms requiring clarification are *stress* and *pressure*. Stress is the physical or mental sensation resulting from a disquieting "internal or external event, force, or condition."[19] An argument with a coworker, a lost set of keys, or worrying about who will cover tonight's evening shift can be stressful. Pressure, on the other hand, involves higher stakes and is "often the source of cognitive and affective discomfort or disorder, as well as maladaptive coping strategies."[20] A job interview at a prestigious law firm, applying to a top-ranked graduate program, or outrunning a hungry grizzly represent pressure. (The first two because of the emphasis you have placed on them, the latter because you might become a bear's dinner!) In *Performing Under Pressure*, Hendrie Weisinger and J.P. Pawliw-Fry provide the following distinction:

> In a *stressful* situation, practicing a relaxation technique might help us feel less overwhelmed and help us regain our perspective and composure. In a pressure moment, relaxing might help us, but we also have to deliver on the required behavior or we don't advance.[21]

Similar to Weisinger and Pawliw-Fry's 2015 book, Kelly McGonigle released *The Upside of Stress* in the same year. Both books have helped spread the word of worry's advantages. They also point out how important it is to create a positive framework to help deal with pressure, or stress, or worry, or fear (see what I mean about terminology overlap?). In short, we feel pressure because we are uncertain about the outcome of something that is important to us. As McGonigle points out, "You don't stress out about things you don't care about, and you can't create a meaningful life without experiencing some stress."[22]

Terms describing psychologically detrimental excess are *obsessive compulsive disorder (OCD)* and *neuroticism.* OCD involves "recurrent intrusive thought (obsessions) that prompt the performance of neutralizing rituals (compulsions)."[23] In *The Brain Advantage*, Madeleine Van Hecke and her coauthors claim, "People with OCD are plagued with obsessive, unwanted thoughts."[24] They point to the work of Jeffrey Schwartz, research professor of psychiatry at the UCLA School of Medicine, and his use of the term *worry circuit.* Those afflicted with OCD feel powerless when certain stimuli trigger their compulsive behavior, such as the sight of a dirty rag wrongly causing them to clean an already clean house—repeatedly. Although used much too casually in our everyday lexicon, OCD is considered a distinct diagnostic category beyond general anxieties.[25]

Neuroticism, one of the so-called Big Five personality dimensions, most resembles anxiety disorders. Neuroticism is often characterized by "persistent and irrational fears, obsessive thoughts, compulsive acts, dissociative states, and somatic and depressive actions."[26] Low self-esteem, low self-efficacy, and weak performance expectations have also been associated with neuroticism. However, these low expectations have often been found to be poor predictors of actual task behaviors in workgroups.[27]

I fuss over the aforementioned terms because of our culture's insistence on using them with little regard for their true meanings and degrees of intensity. Some examples I'll use going forward are ripe (and at times careless) with these terms. Perhaps you, like me, have used these terms incorrectly as synonyms of each other in the past. However, we must bear in mind that the unintended misuse of these terms compromises their utility and our command of the lexicon.

My task is to communicate the benefits of worry, which mostly accrue when worry is exercised *in moderation*. Severe cases of anxiety, such as GAD, and OCD are not generally productive or performance-enhancing. Overdoing an activity after you have accomplished the objective is not a productive use of effort, resources, or talent. This Goldilocks amount of worry (not too worrisome, not too relaxed) helps us accomplish stretch goals, focus on details, and motivates us to act. Worrying shows concern and care, and if you care about something, it gets attention.

Research Notes on the Psychology of Worry

Several researchers have reported on the positive beliefs about worry held by sufferers of GAD.[28] These positive beliefs about worry include "(1) facilitates problem solving; (2) enhances motivation; (3) protects against negative emotions in the event of a negative outcome; (4) prevents negative outcomes in and of itself; and (5) reflects a positive personality trait (akin to conscientiousness)."[29] Worry has also been rationalized as helpful in lessening guilty feelings, preventing future disappointments, and finding better solutions to problems.[30]

Even if you don't suffer from GAD, you can appreciate the logic behind the above set of beliefs. You may engage in these behaviors yourself (hopefully in moderation and not symptomatic of GAD). For instance, if you have an urge to raise your voice with a customer, you'll likely think about the negative consequences that may result and thus decide not to act on that impulse. You may want an extra dessert after dinner, but guilt-induced worrying and the prospects of unwanted weight gain restrain you. Avoidance behavior kicks in after you process the situation cognitively. Also, worry may be positively reinforced if the worrier perceives it to be effective.[31] Again, for those not suffering from unreasonable or "out of proportion" worry or anxiety (i.e., GAD), this process can be beneficial.

As a research construct, worry has outgrown its early station as an "epiphenomenon of anxiety" and has been empirically linked to procrastination and perfectionism.[32] The need for "elevated evidence requirements" and reluctance to make mistakes may contribute to a worrier's procrastinating behavior. Perfectionism, on the other hand, is indicated by an individual's "excessively high personal standards" and "overly critical" self-evaluation.[33] Importantly, researchers have noted that with regard to perfectionism, "worriers do not want to be the best, they are just afraid of making mistakes."[34] Granted, both procrastination and perfectionism can negatively affect performance by inhibiting decision making and action. However, in moderation (i.e., nonpathological worry), these behaviors can lead to more informed choices and better performance. Notably, procrastination and perfectionism are not necessary for worrying to take place.

A more specific form of worry studied in organizational psychology is *job-specific worry*, defined as the attempt "to engage in mental problem solving on situational job-related issues where the outcome is thought to be uncertain but contains a possibility for negative results."[35] For example, variables that may measure job-specific worries, which are not trait dependent like general worry, may include degree of formal hierarchy, rules, and procedures (which should yield less uncertainty and thus less job-specific worry); high level of personal commitment to the organization (likely resulting in more job-specific worry); and perceived risk on the job (e.g., high probability of belligerent customers would increase job-specific worry).[36]

Findings from a study of 57 Norwegian restaurant managers reinforced the differences between worry as a trait versus the more situational job-specific worry. Examples of survey prompts for job-specific worry included "When at work, I worry about mistakes that I may make" and "How much do you worry that guests may complain."[37] While this study did not include performance metrics, as a customer or shareholder I would want a job-specific worrier running my restaurant. Managers with a keen sense of on-site anticipation may better serve customers. For instance, a more worried manager may more closely monitor the needs of patrons during meal consumption. Incidentally, one survey question asked of the managers was, "Sometimes I stay awake at night worrying about my work." While thankfully the average response for this question was low, it is included in the composite score for the degree of job-specific worry.[38]

Other researchers have demonstrated that the content of presleep worry is "negatively toned" and involves a "broad range of concerns" for both insomniacs and good sleepers.[39] There are commonalities between insomnia and GAD. Research has also shown that "positive beliefs about the benefits of worrying during the presleep period are characteristic of insomnia and may serve to maintain the disorder."[40] Again, my point is worry is beneficial when practiced in moderation. This moderation does not entail presleep fretfulness that inhibits restful sleep and impairs performance during subsequent waking hours.

A pair of Canadian researchers interviewed public sector middle managers on the prospect of transforming "coping or surviving" mechanisms resulting from workplace stress into more positive, thriving behaviors. While this study was qualitative and requires empirical follow-up, the authors foresee a "paradigm shift that views stress as desirable and conductive to optimal performance."[41]

A 2015 longitudinal study of 230 law school graduates reported on their degree of worry (referred to as *anxiety* and *rumination* in the paper) experienced prior to taking the California Bar Exam. After the exam, subjects were surveyed every 2 weeks while they waited for exam results. These researchers based their study on an *uncertainty navigation model*, of which anxiety and rumination are germane to experiencing uncertain waiting periods.[42] The study's authors concluded that "Participants who suffered through a waiting period marked by anxiety, rumination, and pessimism responded more productively to bad news and more joyfully to good news, as compared with participants who suffered little during the wait."[43] Essentially, preparing for the worst helped minimize the impact of bad news and resulted in more delight when the news was good.

Another interesting research phenomenon linked to worry is a self-regulation strategy called *mental contrasting*. Conceptualized by Gabriele Oettingen of New York University and the University of Hamburg, mental contrasting involves the "conjoint elaboration of the positive future and the negative reality [that] makes both future and reality simultaneously accessible."[44]

Practitioners of this technique balance any possible optimism bias with a realistic assessment of the obstacles (e.g., not enough time to complete tasks) likely to be encountered. Expectancies and probabilities are assessed, helping to instruct one's behavior. Mental contrasting is believed to help with goal setting and commitment decisions. In short, it helps you decide what is worthy of your efforts—and your worry.

In a study of 52 German health care personnel managers, Oettingen and her colleagues manipulated one group to use mental contrasting for their *everyday concerns*, while a second group was instructed to indulge (i.e., think only of desired future state). Findings indicated those using mental contrasting "fared better in managing their time and decision-making demands" than the subjects trained to indulge. Furthermore, these results indicate mental contrasting to be a time- and cost-effective method for professionals to manage their daily stresses and demands.[45]

In rebuking the myth that positive thinking is required for breaking bad habits, Oettingen points out that "Positive fantasy is not helpful and may even be hurtful when trying to reach a desired future or fulfill a wish."[46] Related to Oettingen's view of obstacle awareness is the concept of premortem, originally developed by David Klein and further studied by Nobel Prize-winning psychologist Daniel Kahneman. As a way of countering traps inherent in the planning fallacy and optimism bias, a premortem exercise provides pragmatic anticipation of potential downsides. Planning, while vitally important, can lead us to expect only a hoped for or idealized future. Kahneman also speaks of an overconfidence that breeds an *illusion of control*. This self-deception lowers your threat consciousness, thereby reducing your self-justification for worrying. Premortem prepares the individual, or team, to better deal with unwanted threats when they emerge.[47]

Strategizing, Scenario Planning, and What-Ifs

Worry is the basis for many aspects of strategic planning. Every what-if analysis, scenario planning exercise, contingency planning protocol, and strategy-making session essentially involves episodes of thoughtful and systematic worrying.

Should possessing a healthy range of worry be a trait criterion for strategic planners or national security analysts? In his academic essay *Why Worry? The Cognitive Function of Anxiety*, Andrew Mathews states, "People who worry little may simply be those who rarely detect environmental cues signaling potential threat."[48] Obviously these people wouldn't make effective strategic planners or security consultants.

It is precisely the future orientation and uncertainty characterizing worry that makes it so complimentary to scenario building and strategic planning. While scenarios are not forecasts, author and scenario planning consultant Gill Ringland views them as "that part of strategic planning that relates to the tools and technologies for managing the uncertainties of the future."[49] Ringland recommends structured frameworks when brainstorming future opportunities or problems. For example, scenario building should be focused in specific areas (such as manufacturing technology, network of R&D partnerships, or threats to component sourcing) and utilize specific analysis frameworks (such as PEST or simulation programs).[50] Indeed, a more purposeful *worry framework* brings needed discipline and is preferred over an open-ended query of future-oriented apprehension.

Former Shell scenario planner Angela Wilkinson and former Shell executive Roland Kupers pointed out in a 2013 *Harvard Business Review* article that "Scenarios are not predictions but plausible stories about the future. They are designed to help break the habit, ingrained in most corporate planning, of assuming that the future will look much like the present."[51] Indeed, this wariness derived from both the planning fallacy and optimism bias is an important contribution of scenario planning. Wilkinson and Kupers add that "Plausible stories encourage judgement, not just attention to data and other information."[52] Again, this is a manifestation of measured worry that looks at plausible, not impossible, environmental forces that informs senior management to choose among thoughtfully conceived alternatives.

Travis Bradberry, coauthor of *Emotional Intelligence 2.0* and president of TalentSmart, claims what-ifs are counterproductive, "throw fuel on the fire of stress and worry," and cost individuals valuable time. Yet he goes on to state, "Of course, scenario planning is a necessary and effective planning technique. The key distinction here is to recognize the difference between worry and strategic thinking about your future."[53] At the very least I have a semantic disagreement with Bradberry on his labeling of worry as deleterious to strategic thinking. I contend that mild to moderate worry promotes better thinking in strategy formulation. I oppose Bradberry's dismissal of what-ifs and I counter that they are germane to the principles of sound strategic planning.

Mergers and acquisitions represent another area where more prudent worry can bolster results. The majority of mergers are deemed unsuccessful in the long run. Precombination activities often focus too much on the financial aspects of the deal, and not enough on the people part of the union.[54] Much of the worrying done in a merger is by employees fretting that the projected synergies of the deal may include the savings from their soon-to-be eliminated salaries. Additionally, many postmerger survivors are left weary with survivor guilt.[55]

Timothy Galpin, author of *The Complete Guide to Merger and Acquisitions*, refers to the retention of key employees as *re-recruitment*. He claims managers should ask themselves, "Who do I need to worry about on my current team?"[56] Given the driver for a merger is usually numbers oriented, it is no wonder the financial fit gets so much more of the due diligence than the people aspects of the deals.

Management consulting scholar Anthony Buono recommends strategic due diligence throughout the merger process. He points to a checklist to help discipline the acquirer to think [worry] about "nonobvious criteria, such as the target company's talent pool, technical capabilities, its organizational structure, cultural values, and prevailing management philosophy toward decision making."[57]

Also embodying the foundation of uncertainty at the core of worry are warranties and insurance policies. Each time a customer purchases an extended warranty, she is worrying. The warranty is a guarantee for mitigating nervous notions about a product's future performance. The bedrock of the entire global insurance industry, be it automobile, home owners, business, product liability, key personnel, or medical malpractice insurance is, by and large, proactive worrying! Derived from cognitive experience, insurance is a risk leveraging tool based on worrying about possible losses in the future. We pay insurance premiums to minimize risk and alleviate worry.

The paradoxical nature of worry is captured by Francis O'Gorman, as he muses, "The analytical powers of the worrier's mind can be curiously beneficial and, despite everything, the odd basis for a kind of hope about how we might at least try to act by taking everything into account."[58] The danger here, however, is the delusion that we can take *everything* into account when analyzing possible futures. One has to keep constructive worrying confined to the relative and the plausible. Nevertheless, the process of anticipating environmental threats and opportunities provides excellent learning opportunities.

High-Profile Worriers

Intel cofounder and tech guru Andy Grove wrote a worrier's manifesto of sorts for business professionals with his aptly titled *Only the Paranoid Survive*. Grove believed, first and foremost, that a manager must "guard constantly against people's attacks and to inculcate this guardian attitude in the people under his or her management."[59] Indicative of the range of his fears and paranoia, Grove wrote:

> I worry about products getting screwed up, and I worry about products getting introduced prematurely. I worry about factories not performing well, and I worry about having too many facto-ries. I worry about hiring the right people, and I worry about morale slacking off . . . I worry about competitors. I worry about other people figuring out how to do what we do better or cheaper, and displacing us with our customers.[60]

Unlike the motorcycle daredevil Evel Knievel, portrayed in film to have said, "Fear is not a word in my vocabulary,"[61] Andy Grove's advice is riddled with the word fear. Grove uses the f-word as an unambigu-ous synonym for worry. In *Only the Paranoid Survive*, Grove further cautions:

> It is fear the makes me scan my email at the end of a long day, searching for problems: news of disgruntled customers, potential slippages in the development of a new product, rumors of unhap-piness on the part of key employees. It is fear that every evening makes me read the trade press reports on competitors' new devel-opments and leads me to tear out particularly ominous articles to take to work for follow-up the next day. It is fear that gives me the will to listen to Cassandras when all I want to do is cry out, "Enough already, the sky isn't falling," and go home.[62]

Grove saw fear as the "opposite of complacency." In particular, he warned that the most successful firms should be the most worried, since their past and present successes were based on environmental conditions that are no longer relevant as dynamic change occurs continually.[63] So to those with the most to lose, start worrying!

Parallel development paths are common in industry, be it a new product, technology platform, process improvement, or ambitious scientific undertaking. The use of parallel development schemes is a manifestation of worry, especially under highly uncertain and complex conditions. Even confident managers must often hedge their bets with a second or third option to improve their odds of success. One could argue this is a more responsible strategy than "putting all your eggs in one basket" with a singular method.

The legendary Manhattan Project, responsible for the development of the atomic bomb in World War II, provides an excellent case study for the virtues of worry-based parallel development. The project's scientific director, Robert Oppenheimer, utilized a parallel development framework with regard to the project's theoretical underpinning (fission versus fusion); fuel type (uranium versus plutonium); and trigger mechanism (implosion versus "gun trigger").[64]

It appears Oppenheimer fretted about the probabilities of success for each method of constructing an atomic bomb. This led him to hedge his bets by pursuing multiple pathways. Nicely summarized by David Kord Murray in his book *Plan B: How to Hatch a Second Plan That's Always Better Than Your First*, the two fission-related projects resulted in a uranium bomb ("Little Boy") with a gun trigger-type detonator, and a larger, plutonium bomb ("Fat Man") employing an implosion approach for detonation. While both of these bomb projects were successful, the dual efforts utilizing a fission reaction are demonstrative of Oppenheimer's worry and lack of certainty in such a high stakes, time sensitive endeavor. Incidentally, the fusion-based effort, led by Edward Teller, resulted in the development of the more powerful hydrogen bomb years later.[65]

A recent example of executive level worry and concern is evident with Auto Nation CEO Mike Jackson. Always leery of environmental flux and threats, Jackson sees himself as the auto retailer's Chief Risk Officer. Even as he described the economy as ideal, Jackson unabashedly proclaimed,

"I'm a big worrier."[66] Constant diligence and market surveillance, combined with healthy amounts of worry help prepare the auto retailer for market opportunities as well as downturns.

The Boom in Antiworry: Is Mindfulness Overrated?

There has been an increase in the adoption of mindfulness practices over the last several years. Meditation and yoga, for example, have gained favor as ways to clear the mind and offer employees a respite from the vexations of the hectic, day-to-day grind. Former Medtronic CEO Bill George, now a professor of management practice at Harvard Business School, lauds mindfulness as a way to "cast off the many trivial worries that once possessed [him]." George contends these techniques improve leadership ability by increasing clarity and removing "needless worries about unimportant things."[67] Salesforce.com founder and CEO Marc Benioff is planning *mindfulness zones* for employee respites within his headquarters building. He recounts a suggestion from Buddhist monks to turn an entire floor in a quiet floor. And while speaking about the importance of corporate philanthropy, Benioff stated, "It's an anxious era. The antidote to anxiety is mindfulness."[68]

David Brendel, a physician and executive coach, considers mindfulness techniques very effective for his clients to "manage stress, avoid burnout, enhance leadership capacity, and steady their minds when in the midst of making important business decisions, career transitions, and personal life changes." However, in a 2015 *Harvard Business Review* piece, Brendel warns of a "cult of mindfulness" that may lead to misuse of otherwise effective techniques.[69]

For instance, Brendel points to a problematic tendency for some to rely on mindfulness as an escape route from difficult decision making or other arduous management duties. Insightfully, Brendel emphasizes how " . . . some problems require more thinking, not less. Sometimes stress is a signal that we need to consider our circumstances through greater self-reflective thought, not a 'mindful' retreat to focused breathing or other immediate sensory experiences."[70]

According to Willoughby Britton, professor of psychiatry at Brown University Medical School, "widespread implementation [of meditation] is premature." Britton cautions that the adoption of meditation by the public and a growing cadre of corporate wellness programs are "outpacing the scientific research." David Gelles, author of *Mindful Work: How Meditation is Changing Business from the Inside Out*, acknowledges the skepticism but touts the growing number of onsite company-sponsored yoga and meditation offerings from progressive firms like Aetna.[71]

The Economist commented on western capitalism's voracious interest in eastern mysticism with the following:

> The biggest problem with mindfulness is that it is becoming part of the self-help movement – and hence part of the disease that it is supposed to cure. Gurus talk about "the competitive advantage of meditation." Pupils come to see it as a way to get ahead in life. And the point of the whole exercise is lost.[72]

I imagine there are managers in organizations that are well resourced and staffed with experienced and motivated professionals that may not see the virtue in worry. Perhaps you own the market you serve by having a dominant, protected position. You may not be forced to constantly do more with less. You may be a uniquely qualified professional with a rare skill set with no cares regarding job security, at least for now.

Yet competitive industries today require personal and organizational betterment. Managers should always be a bit leery when subordinates complete tasks at light speed. Some level of apprehensive suspicion should surface when work gets done just for the sake of being done, and not for excellence. Perhaps we'll find better ways to accomplish difficult tasks that don't signal worry, stress, or pressure. I look forward to more research in mindfulness and organizational psychology that will improve our lives and work performance. But until then . . .

Contra Maxims for Worrying

Be critically optimistic. Sweat the details. Prudent worry is good for business. Worry smartly, not needlessly. Healthy paranoia keeps you and your organization sharp. Practice diligent due diligence. If details matter, hire worriers.

Notes

1. Dale Carnegie, *How to Stop Worrying and Start Living* (New York, NY: Pocket Books, 1985), originally published in 1944.

2. Francis O'Gorman, *Worrying: A Literary and Cultural History* (New York, NY: Bloomsbury, 2015); Zondervan Corporation, *Bible Gateway*, www.biblegateway.com (accessed Nov 23, 2015). For a comparison of the degree of difference in Bible versions, note the following interpretations of Job 5:2, found in the Old Testament: "For wrath killeth the foolish man, and envy slayeth the silly one." (*King James Version*); compare with the *Good News Translation* version of "To worry yourself to death with resentment would be a foolish, senseless thing to do."

3. Merriam-Webster's Collegiate Dictionary, 11th ed. (Springfield, MA: Merriam-Webster, Inc., 2003). s.v. "worry."

4. George Mason University, *Open Source Shakespeare: An Experiment in Literary Technology*, www.opensourceshakespeare.com (accessed Nov 23, 2015); O'Gorman, *Worrying: a Literary and Cultural History*.

5. George Mason University, *Open Source Shakespeare*.

6. O'Gorman, *Worrying: a Literary and Cultural History*.

7. Ibid., 22

8. Ibid., 86

9. Ibid., 87

10. American Psychiatric Association, *Diagnostic and Statistical Manual of Mental Disorders, 5th ed.* (Arlington, VA: American Psychiatric Association, 2013), http://0-dx.doi.org.lib.rivier.edu/10.1176/appi.books.9780890425596 (accessed Nov 10, 2015).

11. Svein Larsen, Torvald Ogaard and Einar Marnburg, "Worries in Restaurant Managers," *Scandinavian Journal of Psychology* 46, no. 1 (2005): 92.

12. Colette Hirsch, Sarra Hayes, Andrew Mathews, Gemma Perman and Tom Borkovec, "The Extent and Nature of Imagery During Worry and Positive Thinking in Generalized Anxiety Disorder," *Journal of Abnormal Psychology* 121, no. 1 (2012): 239.

13. Andrew Mathews, "Why Worry? The Cognitive Function of Anxiety," *Behaviour Research and Therapy* 28, no. 6 (1990): 457.

14. American Psychiatric Association, *Diagnostic and Statistical Manual of Mental Disorders, 5th ed.*

15. Mathews, "Why worry?" 457.

16. Harriett Lerner, "Fear vs. Anxiety," *Psychology Today*, 11 Oct 2009, https://www.psychologytoday.com/blog/the-dance-connection/200910/fear-vs-anxiety (accessed Nov 8, 2015).

17. American Psychiatric Association, *Diagnostic and Statistical Manual*

18. Ibid.

19. G.R. VandenBos (Ed.), *APA Dictionary of Psychology, 2nd ed.* (Washington, DC: American Psychological Association, 2015), 1036–1037, http://0-www.ebrary.com.lib.rivier.edu

20. Ibid., 827

21. Hendrie Weisinger and J.P. Pawliw-Fry, *Performing Under Pressure: The Science of Doing Your Best When it Matters Most* (New York, NY: Crown Business, 2015), 39.

22. Kelly McGonigle, *The Upside of Stress: Why Stress is Good for You, and How to Get Good at It* (New York, NY: Avery, 2015), xxii.

23. VandenBos, *APA Dictionary of Psychology, 2nd ed.*, 725.

24. Madeleine Van Hecke, Lisa Callahan, Brad Kolar and Ken Paller, *The Brain Advantage: Becoming a More Effective Leader Using the Latest Brain Research* (New York, NY: Prometheus, 2010), 224.

25. VandenBos, *APA Dictionary of Psychology, 2nd ed.*, 725.

26. Ibid., 705

27. Corinne Bendersky and Neha Parikh Shah, "The Downfall of Extraverts and Rise of Neurotics: The Dynamic Process of Status Allocation in Task Groups," *Academy of Management Journal* 56, no. 2 (2013): 387–406.

28. Mark Freeston, Josee Rheaume, Helene Letarte, Michel Dugas, and Robert Ladouceur, "Why Do People Worry?" *Personality and Individual Differences* 17, no. 6 (1994): 791–802; Elizabeth Hebert, Michel Dugas, Tyler Tulloch and Darren Holowka, "Positive Beliefs About Worry: A Psychometric Evaluation of Why Worry-II," *Personality and Individual Differences* 56 (2014): 3–8; Michel Dugas and Naomi Koerner, "Cognitive-behavioral Treatment for Generalized Anxiety Disorder: Current Status and Future Directions," *Journal of Cognitive Psychotherapy: An International Quarterly* 19, no. 1 (2005):

61–81; Adrien Wells, "The Metacognitive Model of GAD: Assessment of Meta-worry and Relationship with DSM-IV Generalized Anxiety Disorder," *Cognitive Therapy and Research*, 29, no. 1 (2005): 107–121.

29. Hebert et al., "Positive Beliefs About Worry," 3.
30. Freeston, et al., "Why Do People Worry?;" Larsen, et al., "Worries in Restaurant Managers."
31. Hebert, et al., "Positive Beliefs About Worry"
32. Joachim Stober and Jutta Joormann, "Worry, Procrastination, and Perfectionism: Differentiating Amount of Worry, Pathological Worry, Anxiety, and Depression," *Cognitive Therapy and Research* 25, no. 1 (2001): 49. Note: The methodology described this paper included a gender-skewed sample of 180 students (136 females, 44 males). The authors claim there were no correlation differences between the two groups (p. 58).
33. Ibid., 50
34. Ibid., 57
35. Larsen, et al., "Worries in Restaurant Managers," 92.
36. Ibid.
37. Ibid., 93
38. Ibid.
39. Allison Harvey, "Beliefs About the Utility of Presleep Worry: An Investigation of Individuals with Insomnia and Good Sleepers," *Cognitive Therapy and Research* 27, no. 4 (2003): 404.
40. Ibid., 403
41. Jennifer Walinga and Wendy Rowe, "Transforming Stress in Complex Work Environments," *International Journal of Workplace Health Management* 6, no. 1 (2013): 66.
42. Kate Sweeny, Chandra Reynolds, Angelica Falkenstein, Sara Andrews and Michael Dooley, "Two Definitions of Waiting Well," *Emotion*, 2015, 2, (Advance online publication), http://dx.doi.org/10.1037/emo0000117
43. Ibid., 1
44. Gabriele Oettingen, Doris Mayer and Jennifer Thorpe, "Self-regulation of Commitment to Reduce Cigarette Consumption: Mental Contrasting of Future with Reality," *Psychology and Health* 25, no. 8 (2010): 962.

45. Gabriele Oettingen, Doris Mayer, and Babette Brinkmann. "Mental Contrasting of Future Reality: Managing the Demands of Everyday Life in Health Care Professionals," *Journal of Personnel Psychology* 9, no. 3 (2010): 138.

46. Alina Tugend, "Turning a New Year's Resolution into Action with the Facts," *The New York Times*, 10 Jan 2015, B4.

47. Daniel Kahneman, *Thinking, Fast and Slow* (New York, NY: Farrar, Straus and Giroux, 2011).

48. Mathews, "Why worry?" 57.

49. Gill Ringland, *Scenario Planning: Managing for the Future, 2nd ed.* (Chichester, UK: Wiley & Sons, 2006), 4.

50. Ibid., Note: PEST is an acronym for Political/legal/regulatory, Economic, Sociocultural, and Technological. PEST is a commonly used framework for strategic environmental analysis.

51. Angela Wilkinson and Roland Kupers, "Living in the Futures: How Scenario Planning Changed Corporate Strategy," *Harvard Business Review* 91, no. 5 (May 2013): 121.

52. Ibid., 122

53. Travis Bradberry, "Painful, Valuable Lessons from Taking Charge of My Career," *Pulse*, 11 Nov 2015, https://www.linkedin.com/pulse/boss-painful-valuable-lessons-from-taking-charge-my-career-bradberry (accessed Nov 12, 2015).

54. Mitchell Lee Marks and Philip Mirvis, "Making Mergers and Acquisitions Work: Strategic and Psychological Preparation," *Academy of Management Executive* 15, no. 2 (2001): 80–92.

55. Grainne Collins and James Wickham, "Experiencing Mergers: A Woman's Eye View," *Women's Studies International Forum* 25, no. 5 (2002): 573–583.

56. Kelley Holland, "Under New Management; Life after a Merger: Learning on Both Sides," *The New York Times*, 24 Jun 2007, http://query.nytimes.com/gst/fullpage.html?res=9404EEDA1731F937A15755C0A9619C8B63 (accessed Nov 27, 2015).

57. Anthony Buono, "Consulting to Integrate Mergers and Acquisitions," In L. Greiner & F. Poulfelt (Eds.) *Handbook of Management Consulting: The Contemporary Consultant* (pp. 229–249) (Mason, OH: South-Western, 2005), 236.

58. O'Gorman, *Worrying: A Literary and Cultural History*, xiv

59. Andy Grove, *Only the Paranoid Survive: How to Exploit the Crisis Points that Challenge Every Company* (New York, NY: Currency, 1993), 3.

60. Ibid.

61. *Evel Knievel*, Dir. Marvin Chomsky, (1971; Fanfare Films).

62. Grove, *Only the Paranoid Survive,*118.

63. Ibid.

64. David Kord Murray, *Plan B: How to Hatch a Second Plan that's Always Better than Your First* (New York, NY: Free Press, 2011).

65. Ibid.

66. *Squawk Box*, "CNBC," 2 Apr 2015.

67. Bill George, "Mindfulness Helps You Become a Better Leader," *Harvard Business Review*, 26 Oct 2012, https://hbr.org/2012/10/mindfulness-helps-you-become-a&cm_sp=Article-_-Links-_-End%20of%20Page%20Recirculation (accessed Sep 26, 2015).

68. Quentin Hardy, "He Gave at the Office," *The New York Times*, 8 Nov 2015, F8.

69. David Brendel, "There are Risks to Mindfulness at Work," *Harvard Business Review*, 11 Feb 2015, https://hbr.org/2015/02/there-are-risks-to-mindfulness-at-work (accessed Sep 21, 2015).

70. Ibid.

71. David Gelles, "A CEO's Management by Mantra," 1 Mar 2015, *The New York Times*, BU1, 6.

72. *The Economist*, "The Mindfulness Business," 16 Nov 2013, 73.

CHAPTER 5

Failure is Not an Option

If a machine is expected to be infallible, it cannot also be intelligent.
—Alan Turing

For the loser now will be later to win.
—Bob Dylan, "The Times They Are a-Changin'"

Awash in failures are we. Some are cataclysmic, lots of them inconsequential, and many are natural iterations of works-in-progress. We continually bear witness to failure in life, industry, sports, politics, film, and literature. American novelist John Updike, most known for his *Rabbit* book series, once said, "My characters are all failures."[1]

In *To Engineer is Human: The Role of Failure in Successful Design*, author Henry Petroski points to design failure as the reason for major structural catastrophes such as collapsed bridges and buildings. He believes there is more to learn from structural and mechanical disasters than from the multitudes of successful events and longstanding edifices. Petroski refers to colossal mishaps as unplanned experiments.[2]

We often lose perspective with regard to failure. For instance, if you lose the National Football League's (NFL's) Super Bowl, most fans and media personalities will not consider you a conference champ or the second best team in professional American football. Nay, you lost the Super Bowl. Big game on a big stage. You failed to win. You are a loser! But this is not a recent manifestation of win-or-go-home mentality. Several decades ago John Tunis, a harsh critic of the growing American sports culture, succinctly bemoaned, "Losing is the great American sin."[3]

Tellingly, and more recently, racecar driving caricature Ricky Bobby (played by Will Farrell in the film *Talladega Nights*) bloviated, "If you ain't first, you're last!" While said comically, that statement reads as prudent philosophical wisdom to many. Second place is often seen as the first loser. Our culture seems to collectively swell with a winner-take-all mindset.

America loves a good comeback story though, enjoying the spectacle of an instant mythological phoenix rising above its folly. Our folkloric reversals of failure include General Douglas MacArthur's triumphant return to The Philippines in WWII, and the irascible yet brilliant Steve Jobs' comeback coronation at Apple. Politics is rife with examples of early defeats prior to political stardom. Consider Ronald Reagan's losses for the Republican presidential nomination in 1968 and 1976, Richard Nixon's failed 1962 California Governor's race and loss to John F. Kennedy in 1960, and Bill Clinton's failed 1974 Congressional attempt and unsuccessful 1980 re-election bid as Arkansas Governor.

Power plants, spacecraft, and computer systems all have redundant systems and secondary procedures. Automobiles automatically reduce power to the engine in the event of low oil pressure. Millions of home owners and businesses harbor back-up generators. We use the term *fail-safe* to legitimize our complacency with the workings of all things mechanical, process, behavioral, and nuclear weaponry. The more complex and sophisticated our systems become, the more we need fail-safes for the fail-safes, redundancies for the redundancies.

You probably enjoyed watching the heroics portrayed in the film *Apollo 13*. Following a near catastrophic explosion in outer space, mission coordinator Gene Kranz (played by Ed Harris) barks out the catchphrase, "Failure is not an option!" Ironically it is then a series of failures in the simulator that creates a procedure to help save the astronauts. The iconic coach Vince Lombardi is remembered for, "Show me a good loser and I'll show you a loser." We are conflicted with mixed messages from the zeitgeist buttressed by the idealism of the American Dream. Those in the glass half-full camp take solace in Tennyson's "Tis better to have loved and lost [failed] than to have never loved at all," or the more pedestrian, "For those who don't succeed, try, try again."

The impetus for attacking the flawed maxim *Failure is not an option* is rooted in a recurring phenomenon in business: the majority of new product projects and business start-ups will fail. Reported failure rates of new products vary widely (35–90 percent) depending on definition and methodology. Failures related to canceled new product concepts and programs prior to market launch are extremely common given that numerous concepts never progress beyond the prototype stage. But failure rates for commercially released products are more reasonable, with credible research pegging the failure rate at 40 percent after 3 years on the market.[4] For new companies, the Small Business Administration reports that "About half of all new establishments survive five years or more and about one-third survive 10 years or more."[5] Venture capitalists routinely watch investments go bust or perform poorly while hoping for oversized payouts from just 10 to 20 percent of their speculative litter. Harvard Business School's Shikhar Ghosh claims three-fourths of venture capital backed start-ups don't *succeed*, meaning they don't return invested capital.[6] David Sze, partner at Silicon Valley venture capital firm Greylock Partners, claims, "If you're not making mistakes, you're not doing your job." Bear in mind Greylock invested early in Facebook, LinkedIn, Airbnb, Instagram, and DropBox.[7] Not a bad list of winners.

Pharmaceutical companies, when defending their pricing of proprietary compounds, point to the high cost of drug development as well as the high failure rate on the way to commercialization. For example, Pfizer spent $800 million on a cholesterol treatment named torcetrapib before canceling the program.[8]

Knowing the improbable odds for success, why would a country full of smart managers, entrepreneurs, bankers, investors, inventors, and the employees working on these fledging enterprises devote their resources and careers to inherently risky undertakings? Would a risk premium exist if *Failure was not an option*? I think not.

Go Ahead and Flop

For a historical perspective, Scott Sandage presents a thoughtful recounting of America's public discourse on failure in his book *Born Losers*. In particular, Sandage examines American attitudes toward failure throughout the 19th century. The 1800s witnessed failure and its synonyms become necessary and prevalent in the new capitalist lexicon. Citing the country's surge through adolescence, Sandage reflects:

To a nation on the verge of anointing individualism as its creed, the loser was simultaneously intolerable and indispensable. Failure was the worst thing that could happen to a striving American, yet it was the best proof that the republican founders had replaced destiny with merit.[9]

The 19th century hosted numerous collective failures such as the Depression of 1819 and the economic panics of 1837, 1857, 1873, and 1893. In the wake of the financial panic of 1837, failures were often attributed to character flaws, as Sandage notes:

> The rhetoric of moralists and business leaders quarantined failure like a plague. The whole community had sinned and must atone, but ruined men were the *causes* of pestilence, not its casualties. Theirs was a solitary affliction, contracted through individual error and excess; and it must be contained to avert further outbreak.[10]

America's appetite for growth and adventure gave rise to a masculine, "go-ahead" spirit. Advancing the machismo theme, men with "spunk" were said to have "delivered" while those that blundered had "miscarried." In the mid-19th century, failure was viewed more as "deficiency rather than catastrophe, absence not mischance."[11]

Citing numerous pop culture symbols of failure and the pressure to achieve, Sandage ends the richly detailed *Born Losers* with an emphatic thud, deriding, "Failure is not the dark side of the American Dream; it is the foundation of it. The American Dream gives each of us the chance to be a born loser."[12] I guess I'll never quite look at a newborn baby quite the same ever again. Nevertheless, Sandage's exclamation and his entire treatise on failure are sobering and insightful. America's economic success has much to do with this go-aheadism that is ingrained in the core of American ideals. We romanticize about the fitful growth spurt and scraped knees of a young up-and-coming nation. But the pressure to succeed within a constantly demanding marketplace makes for an environment ripe with angst, uncertainty, and pending doom—regardless of whether you are consciously undertaking risks. This go-ahead spirit lives today with new high-tech fortunes, biotech advances, and privately funded rockets soaring into space. Perhaps the only way to a more advanced future is via this messy acceleration and its concomitant jet wash of failures.

But let's not get too invested in the gloomy, self-fulfilling prophecy of failure and its blame-infested bleakness. We should look at failure as a cognitive, bettering event. Even great offensive football teams fail to gain yardage once in a while, and championship teams in all sports lose an occasional game now and again. Take baseball for instance, dominant teams in Major League Baseball lose more than a third of their games in a season. Baseball's Hall of Fame is teeming with players that failed in 70 percent of their at-bats, although their failures are relatively rare compared to the mere mortals who fared much worse.

The modern American view on failure is somewhat confounded. On one hand we praise the human spirit for trying, even in the face of overwhelming odds. There is nobleness in our wildly optimistic aspirations and fruitless efforts. The loveable loser we can all relate to. Think Charlie Brown of the *Peanuts* comic strip, or Otis the town drunkard in *The Andy Griffith Show*. The iconic little tramp of Charlie Chaplin, struggling against all odds, was emblematic of the everyman's 20th-century effort to just try and keep up with industrialization and prosperity.

America's unique history, culture, and economic ways foster a high tolerance for risk and a selective, conditional attitude toward failure. When comparing the strength of the U.S. economy to much of the world, *Bloomberg Businessweek's* economics editor Peter Coy recently remarked that "The secrets of America's success are flexibility and the willingness to experiment and learn from mistakes."[13] Echoing that sentiment was billionaire venture capitalist Jim Breyer, who while pondering the international envy for America's Silicon Valley, remarked, "There's a magic. There's a love for entrepreneurship and experimentation. . . ." Breyer acknowledges the environmental value of a probusiness culture and vibrant universities, but he sees much of the innovation and risk taking occurring at the grass roots level.[14] Indeed, American tolerance for uncertainty and failure is a competitive advantage, and arguably an intangible national treasure.

Another example of Silicon Valley perseverance and environmental advantage is that of PayPal cofounder and former Yahoo! director Max

Levchin. After four failed start-up attempts, Levchin serendipitously came across Peter Thiel giving a summer lecture on currency trading at Stanford. He only attended the lecture as a respite from the hot Palo Alto climate. Levchin and Thiel met, set a breakfast date, and discussed starting PayPal.[15] As luck would have it, the rest is history. Max Levchin would likely subscribe to Ralph Waldo Emerson's hopefulness, epitomized by, "Our greatest glory is not in never failing, but in rising up every time we fail."

Columbia Business School's Rita Gunther McGrath sees the occasional failure as a given for firms engaged in an experimental orientation as they seek market advantages and continued growth. Indeed, she encourages firms to embrace failure, seeing it as a natural by-product of a quickened decision process. McGrath claims that "Prediction and being 'right' will be less important than reacting quickly and taking corrective action."[16] So initially, being close enough is probably good enough, as long as the organization tweaks, alters, intensifies, or even aborts activities as quickly as possible.

In contrast to this discovery-oriented modus operandi that seeks opportunity while readily absorbing occasional failures, many see failure as the devil incarnate. The f-word shall not be spoken. *Failure is not an option*. Legendary UCLA college basketball coach John Wooden once proclaimed, "If you don't have time to do it right, when will you have time to do it over?" OK, fair point if you are taking a last second jump shot to win a game, and you are only thinking in terms of that particular moment. But what about the next game, or next shot(s). Surely we can get better, we can learn from failed attempts. Maybe we'll even practice our shooting more.

In business, there is usually a next time. A second or third revision of a product or coding sequence that gets it right, makes something better or more competitive. There is always another customer to call on, another pitch. But these revisions must happen quickly. And with all due respect to Coach Wooden (universally revered as a person and a coach), he didn't have much experience with failure. With a career winning percentage of .804 and a record 10 national championships, Coach Wooden was exceptional.[17]

Years ago I worked with a R&D director who said to me during pre-market testing of a new product, "Boy, we could engineer this system like crazy and make it flawless, but by then the market opportunity will have passed us by." He was right. While we would all like to release perfect products, the reality is the marketplace is too dynamic. Additionally, we learn so much more about products and services once mainstream customers start using regularly. Again, if you can move quickly, you can gather feedback and synthesize data from all the microfailures occurring in the field. Then you can improve the value proposition immensely. Unfortunately, in practice this rapid succession of activities is either too slow, inadequately resourced, or poorly executed (or all of the above). Some firms equate a product *release* with a product *finish*. Overconfident and time pressured, management quickly moves on to other projects. Talent and capital are allocated elsewhere and it's on to the next development gig.

Thoughtful Failure

Rapid prototyping prior to full commercialization is essentially a narrowing of the failure profile for a new product or service. Each shortcoming discovered from a subsequent prototype (or test site if a service) leads to further refinement of the finished product. The speed with which this happens is critical. The first few bench models and prototypes are often ridiculously expensive due to low-quantity buys and expedited delivery terms. Early prototypes will most certainly be suboptimal in performance and may even fail outright. But it is worth it given the learning that occurs from every aspect of the product that works well, and more importantly, for every aspect that fails. We learn more from failures than successes. We can isolate the flaws, weak links, and guilty variables. We can anticipate, make necessary changes and proceed. It is important, however, not to favor learning from failure at the expense of learning from success.[18] There should be a balance.

Google's head of people operations, Laslo Bock, lauded the virtues of "rewarding thoughtful failure" in his recent book *Work Rules!* Bock describes how Google's culture is infused with the notion that risk taking is important, and although success is the ultimate goal on every project, failure is expected. Google Wave was an open source e-communication platform that was developed and left on the market for 1 year before being dropped. Despite the project's promise and a talented development team, Google brass decided it was not worth further commercialization efforts. While a bona fide failure in a traditional measurement sense, team members were still rewarded (although not as richly had Google Wave succeeded). Most importantly, other Google employees witnessed the organizational tolerance for failure, which in turn helps inculcate an attitude for healthy risk-taking in Google's culture.[19]

Industries with high product development failure rates, such as toys and pharmaceuticals, need to be particularly attuned to systemically dealing with failure. Indiana University's Dean Shepherd, in his book *From Lemons to Lemonade: Squeeze Every Last Drop of Success Out of Your Mistakes*, insists on normalizing failure. Logically, in environments where experimentation is encouraged, failure will be more common. Shepherd writes, "By normalizing failure, you can enhance persistence with innovation efforts into subsequent projects. It also removes the emotional interference to learning from the failure experience."[20] Another example of conditioning an organization for failure comes from Gill Pratt, former program manager at DARPA (Defense Advanced Research Projects Agency). During a 2016 *Nova* television program covering a DARPA robotics competition, in which more robots failed than succeeded, Pratt exclaimed, "Risking failure is the DARPA way."[21]

Intel's Andy Grove used past failure as a motivator. When recollecting the missteps of the semiconductor giant in the mid-1980s, Grove would summon renewed vigor and passion as a way of guarding against future failures. Intel managers remembered the past pain, and tried hard to avoid those feelings going forward. Grove worked to foster a more open, transparent reporting environment that wouldn't "shoot the messenger" bearing bad news.[22] Granted, senior managers do not like hearing bad news, and they prefer hearing it combined with possible solutions. However, if the solutions are not readily apparent, responsible professionals should make their superiors aware of major failures sooner than later. Quicker disclosure may help refocus available resources toward corrective action.

A high-profile example of commercial failure is that of the Segway motorized scooter. Although still commercially viable, the Segway debacle is centered on prelaunch overhype. An impressive public relations campaign wildly overpromised the product as a revolution in human transport. It obviously failed to live up to these expectations. Segway will likely maintain its niche status in tourism and security patrols. However, a major silver lining in the Segway story is the field experience and reliability data concerning the product's gyroscopic technology. Looking ahead, this technology may have a bright future in products not yet invented.

Research Notes on Enterprise Failure

Marcus Wolfe and Dean Shepherd conducted an interesting study of 66 Division I college football coaches dealing with their first loss of the season. Shepherd and Wolfe studied the *failure narrative* of coaches' post-game press conferences by looking at positive and negative messaging following a loss. They also tested for the presence of an entrepreneurial orientation (EO) of each coach by measuring their degree of risk taking, autonomy, proactiveness, innovativeness, and aggressiveness.[23]

The outcome variable was subsequent performance (in the game after the first loss) measured by point differential. The researchers found both EO and negative emotional content (e.g., press conference filled with negative words) to indicate a U-shaped data curve. This meant performance was high when the negative emotional content and EO were low. Performance was significantly lower when these same influencer variables were more moderate, yet performance was found to be higher again when negative emotional content and EO were highest. In other words, this study found it is better to be a little negative or very negative, but not in between.

Oddly, when positive emotional content was exhibited in the press conferences, an *inverted* U-shaped curve was indicated. This signified subsequent performance was low with both low and high levels of positive EO, but performance was high when moderate amounts of positive EO were present. The results suggests that we need to learn more about finding just the right amount of negativity, positivity, risk taking, autonomy, proactiveness, innovativeness, and aggressiveness in order to positively influence performance, at least on the gridiron.[24]

A 2015 study of Japanese entrepreneurs led by Yasuhiro Yamakawa of Babson College dealt with how entrepreneurs attribute the causes of business failure and thus learn from failure by subsequent sense making of the events. They also studied how persistent (motivated) these entrepreneurs were in overcoming failure (i.e., by starting another venture). Persistence, represented by leading a second or third start-up after failure, is particularly difficult in Japan where culturally it's difficult to attempt even a first shot at venture creation.[25]

Yamakawa and his colleagues recommend entrepreneurs restrain from blaming failures on bad luck or environmental causes. Instead, entrepreneurs need to attribute failures internally to allow learning to occur. The researchers found that entrepreneurs require high levels of intrinsic motivation to overcome previous failures. Lastly, they felt there is a threshold of failure frequency that may affect the entrepreneur, but the *postfailure attitude* is a critical determinant of successful recovery from failure. This recuperation is vital to future new venture attempts.[26]

UK-based research of nearly 600 entrepreneurs led by Deniz Ucbasaran and reported in the *Harvard Business Review* showed 34 percent of repeat entrepreneurs had suffered a failure. Fifty-nine percent of those claiming failure were serial entrepreneurs. While previous failures can be cognitive reality checks to repeat entrepreneurs, overconfidence is more prevalent with serial venture starters than with first timers. The characteristic of supreme confidence is often a double-edged sword. There appears to be an attribution bias with serial entrepreneurs focused solely on one enterprise at a time, at least when compared to portfolio entrepreneurs with a more hedged risk profile consisting of multiple enterprises. Entrepreneurs may be protecting their sense of control and self-esteem by resisting deep reflections of failure.[27] Indeed, when commenting on how attribution bias can inhibit organizational learning, researchers Francesca Gino and Bradley Staats claim, "It is common for people to ascribe their successes to hard work, brilliance, and skill rather than luck; however, they blame their failures on bad fortune."[28]

A study by Jason Cope, Frank Cave, and Sue Eccles in the journal *Venture Capital* looked at attitudes of U.S. and UK venture capitalists toward entrepreneurs with previous failure experience. Cope and his team found additional evidence of a more forgiving mindset toward entrepreneurial failure in the United States than in the United Kingdom. It should also be noted that although a previous failure is not necessarily a demerit, it may be offset by other investment decision criteria such as a compelling product opportunity.[29]

Coming to terms with failure is by no means pleasant. There are numerous reasons why an entrepreneur or project leader would resist the urge to quit on an endeavor or advocate premature closure due to the inability to attain desired results. Antifailure bias and competency traps (e.g., we've been successful previously) can impair management thinking and decision making.[30] Some of the problematic reasons for persisting with a failing project include the following:

- Overconfidence
- Sunk costs
- Perceived need for self-justification
- Denial
- Social cost of admitting failure
- Completion effects
- Exit barriers[31]

Perhaps you have witnessed or experienced some of the above phenomena. I'll admit to all of them, including the thought of abandoning this book project a few times. Yet I pressed on due to potential social costs (I told colleagues about the project); sunk costs (I already spent countless hours on specific research and writing); and overconfidence (it took me twice as long as originally planned).

In contrast to hanging on too long to an undeserving project or enterprise, many managers and entrepreneurs confront their doubts and elect to quit or suspend the endeavor. This lack of persistence may happen even when a thorough analysis may recommend that one should continue instead of quitting. Decisions based on *false negatives* may be attributed to:

- Aversion to loss
- Opportunity costs
- Perceived risk of persistence
- Intolerance of failure
- Publicly stated limits
- Reluctance to renew budget
- Shifting mood and outlook of the organization[32]

Again, rationalizations for curtailing a project or business often have much to do with the perceptions of others, organizational politics, and ego. Thinking can become fuzzy as a project meanders through the middle stages, where the newness has worn off and significant money has been spent with much more needed in order to proceed. The end stages of a project may also cloud decision makers' vison regarding alternative choices and opportunity costs. The closer to completion, the more impactful the project's end game becomes vis-a-vis alternatives.

If We Are So Smart, Why Do We Fail So Often?

An excellent introduction into the cognitive and systemic reasons for failure can be found in Dietrich Dorner's *The Logic of Failure*. Dorner points out how humans constantly struggle with the demands of complex decision making. While intelligent, humans are plagued with slow brains—at least when compared to computers. A coping mechanism for this time constraint is to economize the process for dealing with problems, which often leads to hasty and poor decisions. We fall back to our own mental models and rules of thumb, applying these simplified (and often efficient) frameworks so that we don't have to reinvent the wheel, especially with routine decisions.

Our cognitive process is limited and often sequential. Dorner points out our propensity to use established rules, or methodism, to get things done. He also explains our flawed reasoning for cause and effect:

> We find an inability to think in terms of nonlinear networks of causation rather than chains of causation – an inability, that is, to properly assess the side effects and repercussions of one's behavior. We find an inadequate understanding of exponential development, an inability to see that a process that develops exponentially will, once it has begun, race to its conclusion with incredible speed. These are all mistakes of cognition.[33]

An example of this could be a physician ordering a new prescription that may have serious side effects if taken with a new variety of pain relievers. The physician uses reductive reasoning for solving the original condition, and may not extrapolate the threat manifesting from subsequent drug interactions. Humans often complicate these problems by committing errors of omission. We do not think about problems we do not currently have.

For a business failure example, consider a smart, well-capitalized management team starting a new car manufacturing company. They may not anticipate the rise in car sharing developing from social networking technology. The management team is focused on making performance-oriented automobiles that are very competitive against current models on the market. The new firm is adept at traditional, product-based competition. Management understands the pros and cons of all competitors currently on the market. However, while the firm sees car sharing agencies as potential customers, it may be unprepared if car ownership rates drop precipitously. Hypothetically, 20 percent of current car owners could elect to enroll in car sharing (due to their own poor utilization of a self-owned vehicle), and the number of potential new car purchases could drop significantly.

Dorner uses the 1986 Chernobyl nuclear disaster as an apropos example of failed thinking. He recounts the plant's well-trained operators as a safety award-winning crew trying to perform a test (ironically to improve safety) ordered by headquarters in Moscow. There were numerous opportunities to abort the test—even as warning signs appeared—but politics, overconfidence, energy demand pressure, and established practices contributed to the crew's poor decisions.[34]

Success and failure, like winners and losers, are relative. Mark Twain, himself no stranger to the threats of bankruptcy, once quipped, "Let us be thankful for the fools, but for them the rest of us could not succeed."[35] We tussle with the score-keeping aspect of our commercially driven behavior. Capitalism creates wealth, growth, and bigger pies, but failure looms as a side effect of competition, choice, and the struggle for prosperity.

Bankruptcy is a failure mode shared among individuals, businesses, nonprofit organizations, and governments. *Forbes* recently asked 50 billionaires, of which we would assume that they or someone before them were enormously successful economically, the following question: Have you ever owned a company that went bankrupt? Just 10 percent said yes. *Forbes* also queried these same billionaires with, "Is failure in business inevitable at some point?" Nearly 40 percent responded affirmatively.[36]

Mitigating the Risks of Failure

Trying to anticipate or predict failure can dramatically improve a new product's chances for success. This is also important with regard to product liability for producers, and improved safety for users. Knowing the mean-time-to-failure (MTTF) and mean-time-between-failure (MTBF) for items such as mobile phones, televisions, automobile components, and medical implants (and their components) helps determine performance expectations and warranty periods. Manufacturing firms routinely perform some form of Failure Modes, Effects, and Criticality Analysis (FMECA) on their new products prior to launch. Employees, usually engineers and marketing types, and sometimes customers will get together to perform a FMECA that includes brainstorming different ways a product may malfunction. Probability and severity are assigned to each failure condition. The team then ponders what effect each failure may have on the user, patient, other components, the overall system, and so on. FMECA exercises help spot potential problems before product launch. They are also useful for writing user manuals, crafting warning or cautions statements, and anticipating service needs.

For instance, overheating is a potential failure mode for circuit boards inside laptop computers with the result being a system shutdown. The probability of this failure mode is low, however, and the impact on a user is not life threatening, albeit very annoying. Using pre- and postlaunch performance data, manufacturers can confidently tell when components will fail, making the determination of warranty periods fairly easy. Most failures will thus occur after the factory warranty period has expired.

Electronic device makers have benefited from users craving newness over reliability. User expectations for long-term operation are low to say the least. Smartphones, for instance, don't last much longer than the warranty periods because, quite simply, they don't have to.

As we near the end of our discussion on failure, I hope you can appreciate the benefits of coming up short and learning from mistakes. In his recent book on the importance of failure in science, Columbia University's Stuart Firestein optimistically states, "Science is a series of provincial findings that iteratively moves us closer and closer to a truth that may never be fully attained. But the provisional iterations are valuable even though they are ultimately wrong."[37]

While I like to win and succeed as much as anyone, I too think it is important to maintain perspective on the total effort. The following from Walt Whitman's *Song of Myself* sums this up:

> *Vivas* to those who have failed....
> Have you heard that it was good to gain the day?
> I also say it is good to fall, battles are lost in the same spirit in which
> they are won.[38]

I'll close with one final example. I have a Canadian friend who is an accomplished design engineer. Following a university tradition, he wears a nondescript metal ring on his finger. The ring symbolizes the failure of the Quebec Bridge that collapsed into the St. Lawrence River in 1907. This reminds the wearer of potential failures in their engineering work. That's as good a lesson as any about learning from failure.

Contra Maxims for Failure

Fail small, preferably early, and as rapidly as possible. Keep experimenting and learning from each failure. Prepare to be wrong. Expect and normalize failure. Fail smart!

Notes

1. Scott Sandage, *Born Losers: A History of Failure in America* (Cambridge, MA: Harvard University Press, 2005). Cited by Sandage, from John Updike appearance on *The Charlie Rose Show*, December 22, 1992, WNYC Television, New York.
2. Henry Petroski, *To Engineer is Human: The Role of Failure in Successful Design* (New York, NY: Vintage, 1992), viii.
3. Edward Walsh, "An American Problem: How to Live with Defeat," *The New York Times*, 20 Mar 1977, 174.
4. Eric Anderson, Song Lin, Duncan Simester and Catherine Tucker, "Harbingers of Failure," *Journal of Marketing Research* 52, (Oct 2015): 580–592; George Castellion and Stephen Markham, "Perspective: New Product Failure Rates: Influence of *Argumentum ad Populum* and Self-interest," *Journal of Product Innovation Management* 30, no. 5: 976–979.

5. U.S. Small Business Administration, Office of Advocacy, "Frequently Asked Questions," Sep 2012, https://www.sba.gov/sites/default/files/FAQ_Sept_2012.pdf (accessed Sep 30, 2015).

6. Deborah Gage, "The Venture Capital Secret: 3 Out of 4 Start-ups Fail," *The Wall Street Journal*, 20 Sep 2012, http://www.wsj.com/articles/SB10000872396390443720204578004980476429190 (accessed Oct 1, 2016).

7. BloombergTV, *Studio 1.0*, 2015, Greylock Partners David Sze and John Lilly interviewed by Emily Chang, viewed July 11, 2015.

8. *The Economist*, "Pharmaceuticals: The Price of Failure," 29 Nov 2014, 59.

9. Sandage, *Born Losers*, 27.

10. Ibid., 46.

11. Ibid., 87.

12. Ibid., 278.

13. Peter Coy, "America the Relatively Beautiful," *Bloomberg Businessweek*, 2–8 Feb 2015, 8.

14. *Bloomberg Businessweek*, "Focus on Davos: What's in the innovation sandwich?" 19–25 Jan 2015, 50.

15. BloombergTV, *Studio 1.0*, 2015, Max Levchin interviewed by Emily Chang, viewed Apr 3, 2015.

16. Rita Gunther McGrath, *The End of Competitive Advantage* (Boston, MA: Harvard Business Review Press, 2014), 23.

17. *Biography*, "John Wooden," http://www.biography.com/#!/people/john-wooden-21369183 (accessed Jul 10, 2015).

18. Jason Cope, "Entrepreneurial Learning from Failure: An Interpretive Phenomenological Analysis," *Journal of Business Venturing* 26, no. 6 (2011): 606.

19. Laslo Bock, *Work Rules!: Insights from Inside Google that Will Transform How You Live and Lead* (New York, NY: Twelve, 2015).

20. Dean Shepherd, *From Lemons to Lemonade: Squeeze Every Last Drop of Success Out of Your Mistakes* (Upper Saddle River, NJ: Wharton School Publishing, 2009).

21. WGBH Boston, *Rise of the Robots*, 2016, Nova series, s43, e17.

22. Andy Grove, *Only the Paranoid Survive: How to Exploit the Crisis Points that Challenge Every Company* (New York, NY: Currency, 1999), 119.

23. Marcus Wolfe and Dean Shepherd, "'Bouncing back' from a Loss: Entrepreneurial Orientation, Emotions, and Failure Narratives," *Entrepreneurship Theory and Practice,* (May 2015): 675–700.

24. Ibid.

25. Yasuhiro Yamakawa, Mike Peng and David Deeds, "Rising from the Ashes: Cognitive Determinants of Venture Growth after Entrepreneurial Failure," *Entrepreneurship Theory and Practice,* (March 2015): 209–236.

26. Ibid.

27. Deniz Ucbasaran, Paul Westhead and Mike Wright, "Why Serial Entrepreneurs Don't Learn from Failure," *Harvard Business Review,* (April 2011): 26.

28. Francesca Gino and Bradley Staats, Why Organization Don't Learn," *Harvard Business Review,* (Nov 2015): 110–118.

29. Jason Cope, Frank Cave and Sue Eccles, "Attitudes of Venture Capital Investors Towards Entrepreneurs with Previous Business Failure," *Venture Capital* 6, no. 2–3 (2004): 147–172.

30. Rita Gunther McGrath, "Falling Forward: Real Options Reasoning and Entrepreneurial Failure," *Academy of Management Review* 24, no. 1 (1999): 13–30.

31. Helga Drummond, "Escalation of Commitment: When to Stay the Course," *Academy of Management Perspectives* 28, no. 4 (2014): 431.

32. Ibid.

33. Dietrich Dorner, *The Logic of Failure: Recognizing and Avoiding Error in Complex Situations* (Cambridge, MA: Basic, 1997), 33.

34. Ibid., 28–35.

35. Mark Twain, *Following the Equator, and Anti-Imperialist Essays,* Shelly Fisher Fishkin (Ed.) (New York, NY: Oxford University Press, 1996 [originally published in 1897]), 268.

36. *Forbes,* "LeaderBoard," 29 Jun 2015, 28.

37. Stuart Firestein, *Failure: Why Science is so Successful* (New York, NY: Oxford University Press, 2015), 174.

38. Walt Whitman, "Song of Myself," [1855] in *Leaves of Grass and Other Writings,* Michael Moon (Ed.) (New York, NY: W.W. Norton, 2002), 40. Note: "*Vivas* to those who have failed" is from 1st edition, later revised as "To those who've failed in aspiration vast." [originally published in 1888], 426.

CHAPTER 6

Consensus Decision Making is Optimal

It is the nature of a new idea to confound current consensus—even the mildly new idea . . . the group has a vested interest in its miseries as well as its pleasures, and irrational as this may be, many a member of organization life can recall instances where the group clung to known disadvantages rather than risk the anarchies of change.
—William H. Whyte, *The Organization Man*

I don't believe anything really revolutionary has ever been invented by committee. Because the committee would never agree on it.
—Steve Wozniak, *iWoz*

Decisions, decisions. Making them under complex conditions and with uncertainty is difficult. Arguably, this is where the human brain's cognitive capabilities should shine. Simple decisions can be made without thinking, and executed with a preordained, unconscious decision framework or mental model. Complex decisions, although some need to be done quickly, require deep thinking, information gathering, and analysis. I tell my business students that making tough decisions is a big reason why they'll be employed; otherwise a monkey, machine, or computer algorithm would be doing the job. A task that doesn't require much thinking or judgment most likely doesn't require you!

The question becomes where does industry value decision making as a management virtue? The folks at *Bloomberg Businessweek* polled over 1,300 corporate recruiters concerning the most desired skills for newly minted MBA graduates. Surprisingly, decision making ranked 10th, with just 20 percent of recruiters saying it was one of the top five most important skills. For the record, communication skills ranked first among responding recruiters (with 68 percent listing it as a top five skill), followed by analytical thinking, ability to work collaboratively, strategic thinking, leadership, creative problem solving, motivation/drive, adaptability, and quantitative skills.[1]

Granted, all of these performance traits are admirable, but one would think savvy decision making would rate higher. Perhaps the management profession believes that the propensity to reach consensus will even out any rough spots in a fresh MBA graduate's skill set. Individually, a young executive may struggle with decision making, but as long as he or she is able to collaborate and play nicely with others (e.g., be agreeable on group consensus), all is well. The good news is the more experience-oriented skill of delegating did not make the top 10 MBA virtues. When interviewing job candidates, I would always raise a red flag when young interviewees claimed their top strength was delegating. However, it does sound more positive than the painfully honest reply, "I lack a bias for action so I need to select others to do the actual work." So while delegation may not be in vogue, it can be substituted with collaboration as a convenient way for the less inclined to thrive and take some credit.

Perhaps decision making has taken a back seat due to advances in decision support systems, predictive analytics, and intelligent agents (web bots and such). I would argue the opposite should occur given the now overwhelming amount of data being generated. Intelligence gathering ad nauseam provides the fodder for making more informed judgments and choices. Combine this with the rapid pace of market change and executives must continually refine their thinking and tactics. They must decide quickly, evaluate, and decide again, even if that next decision is to do nothing. Good managers need to do this without convening the team on every decision event. As I'll discuss later in the chapter, group deliberations take valuable time and do not necessarily improve outcomes. But first I'll review some foundational decision concepts.

In his book *Thinking, Fast and Slow*, Nobel Prize-winning psychologist Daniel Kahneman eloquently explains the decision-making process through the lens of two systems, not so eloquently referred to as System

1 and System 2.[2] System 1 is fast, automatic, and emotional. It contains our rules of thumb, those handy nuggets of finely aged wisdom such as looking left-right-left when crossing a street, knowing you should diversify your investment portfolio, and how to effortlessly operate your motor vehicle. However, System 1 is also responsible for many errors due to our reliance on ritualized, outdated rules (e.g., "This is how we've always done it").

System 1 uses our adaptive unconscious. Malcolm Gladwell, in his bestseller *Blink: The Power of Thinking Without Thinking*, lauds the adaptive unconscious for its speed and capability to seamlessly process "glances" in two seconds or less. One of Gladwell's objectives in *Blink* is to convince the reader that "decisions made very quickly can be every bit as good as decisions made cautiously and deliberately."[3]

In contrast to the flashlike process of System 1, System 2 thinking is slower, analytical, and more deliberate. It can often act as a safeguard by inhibiting poorly conceived impulses.[4] We rely on System 2 thinking for the hard choices, at least when we have the time. For example, buying a nonroutine item like a house or car utilizes the System 2 framework. A company's decision to make or buy a component part, if conducted analytically, would also be a System 2 decision. However, if the firm has a cultural norm, rule of thumb or corporate commandment like "Thou shall not perform any manufacturing other than assembly of finished goods," this would likely initiate a quick System 1 decision. Inclinations and emotions can shift into involuntary System 1 rules if they are backed up by System 2 over time.[5] Quick, default decisions built on rules, however informal, are System 1 no brainers. Well, no brainers in the nonliteral sense of course.

While the above serves as a primer on decision making in general, how does it inform a perspective on group decision making? How does it support an assault on the problematic maxim of *Consensus decision making is optimal?*

For starters, consensus is duplicitous. On the plus side, it's a group goal, unanimous agreement, or hard-fought, courageous compromise. It's something you've reached or achieved. It's group solidarity, common ground. It's the prevailing opinion (publically stated, that is). Sometimes it's a necessity, a relief. Former U.S. Senator Olympia Snow once remarked "You can never solve a problem without talking to people with whom you disagree. The United States Senate is predicated and based on consensus building. That was certainly the vision of the founding fathers." Today, on her website dedicated to reducing polarization in Washington, Sen. Snow endorses the position that "Government can work again, but only when Americans support and vote for individuals who will follow the principles of consensus building."[6]

On the not so positive side, a consensus is often a reluctant compromise, an appeasement, something for which you've settled, a bargain between competing interests. It's not usually a hallmark of excellence, and often not the best choice of alternatives. It's not an outright win, but is instead what you get when you're playing not to lose. It's noncommittal, a dressed up stalemate or consolation.

Hardly a fan of consensus, acclaimed author and producer Michael Crichton once snarled, "Historically, the claim of consensus has been the first refuge of scoundrels; it is a way to avoid debate by claiming that the matter is already settled." Former British Prime Minister Margaret Thatcher, the revered Iron Lady, chided consensus as "something in which no one believes and to which no one objects."

Before looking at recent evidence of flawed decision making in group settings, we should review the well-known concept of groupthink. Groupthink was popularized by Irving Janis in the early 1970s. Janis believed groups tended toward consensus, uniformity, and even censorship. He felt groups were more susceptible to groupthink if they were cohesive, insulated from external experts, and led by highly directive leadership. Janis viewed groupthink as a contributor to fiascos such as the lack of preparedness for the attack on Pearl Harbor, the botched Bay of Pigs invasion, and the escalation of the Vietnam War. [7]

Janis presented eight symptoms of groupthink, including the three illusions of invulnerability, morality, and unanimity; along with stereotyping, rationalization, self-censorship, reliance upon self-appointed mindguards, and direct pressure on dissidents.[8] Far from just being nostalgic, I include these eight group-empowered sins as timeless representations of our often timid human nature.

Fast forward roughly 45 years, and we are treated to the 2015 book *Wiser: Getting Beyond Groupthink to Make Groups Smarter*, a solid accounting on the shortcomings of group decision making. In *Wiser*, authors Cass Sunstein and Reid Hastie take advantage of decades of progress in psychology research, including their own experiments. They blame deliberation as an enabler of bad group decisions, largely due to the influence of information signals and social pressures. They also highlight the discouragement of dissension from the group position due to the publically disclosed nature of the group's early stance. Additionally, social pressure keeps members silent, especially in the presence of a strong group leader with clear convictions.[9]

The aforementioned influences of information signals and social pressures can lead to four problems, including the following:

- Amplifying, rather than solving, problems.
- Cascade effects are created, meaning members follow and corroborate early decisions that are wrong, particularly if early contributions are from influential and powerful members.
- Groups become more polarized as subsequent discussions reinforce early stances.
- Groups tend to share and revisit old information. New evidence, especially that which is contradictory to stated group positions, is not given a fair hearing.[10]

Sunstein and Hastie acknowledge that groups can also perform well. Consensus can be appropriate when the early decisions are correct and all members get behind good decisions. Additionally, the use of cross-functional teams brings specific expertise (e.g., cost accounting, code troubleshooting, or material science know-how) to the group which improves group diversity and enhances team performance. Synergy may be realized if divergent thinking and minority views are encouraged.[11]

However, group confidence may grow as a result of deliberation even when the group's position is wrong (and actually believed to be wrong by some members, although they are reluctant to step forward). Thanks in part to social and informational pressures, ". . . .individual biases are not systematically corrected at the group level and they often get worse."[12] This false positive reduces variance within the group and fosters an unhealthy consensus. To make matters worse, overconfidence can set in as the group pressures members to conform and affirm the collective's position.

Not only does extended deliberation cause polarization, but initial group opinions become more severe over time, further restricting opposing viewpoints and challenges by devil's advocates.[13] This snowball effect of conformity squashes dissent and inhibits prospecting for new alternatives.

Sunstein and Hastie also elaborate on three interesting characteristics of the group dynamic: complacency, happy talk, and anxiety. The first two are counterproductive to quality group decisions and contribute to consensus. Group members are often upbeat and confident. The *Wiser* authors point out that "human beings have a pervasive tendency toward unrealistic optimism."[14] The complacent and happy talkers try not to rock the boat, and they speak assuredly as though everything is fine so no one needs to worry. But in reality, everything is not fine. Conformity and the pursuit of group goals combine to exploit the wishful optimism of agreeable group members.

In *Organizing Genius*, Warren Bennis and Patricia Ward Biederman praised what they termed *Great Groups*, including the Manhattan Project and Lockheed's Skunk Works. They cited Great Groups as being "optimistic, not realistic."[15] However, there can be a tendency to lump praise on a collective for decision making when the group is really only responsible for carrying out tasks (although important). One has to look deeply at group member interplay and individual contributions to distinguish between reluctant buy-in and spirited discourse about alternatives.

A pair of Bain & Company consultants once insightfully wrote that "Consensus is a worthy goal, but as a decision-making standard, it can be an obstacle to action or a recipe for lowest-common-denominator compromise." But they digressed by following with "a more practical objective is to get everyone involved to buy in to the decision."[16] The latter statement tries to make a distinction between consensus and buy-in, but instead only heralds the ideal of being good team players. The point here is there can be unintended consequences of esprit de corps. A group stacked with too much kumbaya and unbridled optimism can be a mixed blessing.

Members often agree to disagree, even if only implicitly. As a young and naïve manager I recall feeling professionally bullied to agree to a previously unacceptable manufacturing schedule. I responded to this pressure with a bewildered silence (of which I was not proud). My over-confident program leader had political clout and happy talked his way through status meetings with the brass. The results were unfulfilled orders and a very unpleasant backlash from upper management who felt betrayed. Lesson learned—the hard way.

Anxious people, on the other hand, are always challenging the status quo and worried about what can go wrong. These are the much needed (but underappreciated) devil's advocates, doubters, realists, wet blankets, and frequently real downers. But they make outcomes better. Anxious people "see obstacles, downsides, and challenges everywhere."[17] These agitating folks are committed to team success, but they are certainly not complacent or happy talkers. Every group should have some degree of anxiety.

The CEO of Catholic Health Initiatives, Kevin Lofton, was asked what was unusual about his company's culture. His response centered around the use of a devil's advocate at senior management meetings to mitigate the chances of groupthink on critical issues. While it's encouraging to hear a large firm (over 100 hospitals nationwide) routinely employ the devil's advocate technique, it's also discouraging because the CEO was responding to a query of "what's *unusual* about the culture."[18] Granted, overuse of devil's advocacy can lead to chronic negativity, but many organizations shy away from useful exercises that often provoke a more balanced analysis. Some tout the wearing of black hats for the role-playing dissenters, providing both a visual cue for the role and a free pass to voice politically incorrect or divergent viewpoints. Say something unpopular or counter to the prevailing opinion? Just blame it on the hat.

Another interesting method for averting poor group performance is called a *premortem*, introduced by psychologist Gary Klein. Just prior to implementing a decision, a group convenes under the assumption that the proposed decision turned out to be a real dud in a hypothetical future. Each group member writes a brief story recounting how and why the hypothetical disaster happened. Two benefits of this approach are that it helps to overcome groupthink and it gives permission for individuals to think deeper and more freely about alternative solutions.[19]

Some group members resist devil's advocacy exercises because they just want to finish the project. They have no interest in unearthing more problems. They seek concurrence and a united front. They long for a group consensus that validates that the group finished the job! A good way to deal with this is to link group member rewards to field outcomes some time into the future, maybe 6 months after product launch. Team members should be partially rewarded for postproject field performance (if measurable) and not just a checked box showing that a project was completed. Groups should strive for a balance of completion and quality outcomes.

Digital Mob as Group Force

Intriguing group dynamics are being played out on social media platforms such as Twitter, Facebook, Instagram, LinkedIn, and a bevy of lesser known wikis, blogs, and web forums. I'll pick on Twitter due to its ubiquity and shallowness. For instance, when watching a video news story you'll likely notice the broadcast sometimes includes tweets on the topic. These tweets are from random viewers, opinion givers, or attention seekers. I am not sure if I am more annoyed or perplexed at this development. While the quality of so-called news has become more diluted of late, I still look to specific sources for objective, disinterested accounts of what is going on in the world. I don't particularly care what #sluggo@ moonbase9r thinks about the latest bilateral nuclear treaty, or the global debt crisis *du jour*. One can begin to see how clumps of trite online comments can mass into a common theme that may increase conformity in public opinion.

How does this help the community consider issues? Does it widen or deepen group discourse to any meaningful extent? James Surowiecki's book *The Wisdom of Crowds* speaks to the ability of crowds to answer fact-based queries with astonishing accuracy. Examples include estimating the weight of farm animals, determining a room's temperature, and guessing the dates of historical events. On average, the crowd is often found to be more accurate than individual experts. Surowiecki points out that polling the audience on the game show *Who Wants To Be A Millionaire* yields an impressive 91-percent success rate, while the phoning a friend option is correct 65 percent of the time.[20] Interestingly, audience members answer questions largely independently, without deliberation. Speaking more generally, Surowiecki adds, "Diversity and independence are important because the best collective decisions are the product of disagreement and contest, not consensus or compromise."[21]

For more complex, open-ended decision criteria, the crowd is far less effective. A major drawback of the digital mob is the reinforcement of halo effects and false positives. Although the Internet has helped democratize the speech and reach of countless millions, it has manifested patterns of groupthink within the mainstream. The smaller, dissenting voices are largely ignored and buried in obscure blog responses. Our by-line populism does little to advance real engagement or debate, especially if done in fewer than 140 characters.

Mark Klein, of MIT's Center for Collective Intelligence (CCI), claims social media platforms produce "more heat than light" when used for complex decision-making needs. Problem-solving difficulties for e-crowds include disorganized and highly redundant content; lots of contributions with little depth; polarization and self-assembly of the like-minded; and dysfunctional argumentation that favors bias over evidence.[22] Additionally, standard online forums typically organize discussions within a time orientation and suffer from a soapbox effect (i.e., last to speak). The soapbox effect overemphasizes more recent and redundant postings.[23]

A more deliberative approach is required for complex, open-ended problem-solving efforts to be effective online. The online crowd needs participants that are properly motivated, independent, and apprised of the subject matter. In other words, the online crowd needs to be qualified. Emerging is a promising development called *collaborative deliberation*, defined as the "systematic exploration, evaluation, and convergence on solution ideas."[24] Developed as part of MIT's Deliberatorium project, an online argument mapping tool seeks to improve large-scale deliberation of complex problems. Argument mapping organizes content by problem (not by time), which then welcomes ideas or problem-solving approaches that prompt arguments for or against the ideas. Postings are rated and moderating is required, but there is no repetition or scattering of content. Bias is toward collaboration and better arguments. Additionally, the tool takes more advantage of the long tail effect, increasing the diversity of thinking and *small voice* contributions from the tail end of the frequency distribution.[25] Go online and check it out!

Boards will be Boards

The corporate board of directors (BOD) represents a well-known form of high-level group decision making. BODs are responsible for corporate governance, hiring and evaluation of the chief executive, fiduciary oversight and integrity of financial statements, monitoring company performance, and, of course, representation of the stockholders' best interests. Dartmouth's Sydney Finkelstein, along with Ann Mooney of the Stevens Institute of Technology, suggested five goals to which boards should aspire in order to increase board performance (i.e., make good decisions). These goals include the following:

- Engage in constructive conflict (especially with the CEO)
- Avoid destructive conflict
- Work together as a team
- Know the appropriate level of strategic involvement
- Address decisions comprehensively

Additionally, Finkelstein and Mooney stressed the importance of selecting the right people for the board.[26] Management scholars at Penn State University recently suggested a model for corporate director effectiveness that stressed a director's independence, expertise, motivation, and bandwidth.[27] Having served on a public firm's board for several years, I would concur with the emphasis on good judgment, experience, and a willingness to speak one's mind as important for board composition. But even at senior executive levels it takes courage to buck the majority decision. There is not only a social price to potentially pay, but the dissenter often doubts their contrary position.[28] Furthermore, directors are usually very busy people. Their time constraints (lack of bandwidth) can influence reluctant agreement and result in consensus.

In the book, *The CEO's Boss*, Columbia Business School's William Klepper recommends a social contract to guide the priorities of directors, ensuring alignment with company values and strategies. Sounds good, but Klepper also touts consensus as a way of encouraging cooperation among directors.[29] I agree that there is a strong link between cooperation and consensus. Unbridled cooperation may be the mother's milk of consensus. Again, while harmonious, this does not produce optimal decision making. It promotes *agreeable* group decision making, which should not be the objective.

BODs have taken heat over the years for falling prey to the ills of group decision making. Social pressures within the group are particularly troublesome given that board selection is often accomplished by personal or professional networks of incumbent directors or management. This is not a sinister phenomenon but one of trust and familiarity. For example, a senior manager or director vouches for a board candidate's character, intellect, and expertise. Yet problems may arise due to implicit reciprocity demands or conformity bias that may contribute to unwise consensus down the road.

Are Diversity and Consensus Inherently Disharmonious?

Two of the most sought after attributes in organizations today are diversity and consensus building. Both of these ideals are lavished with positive media commentary and academic study. However, one wonders if added diversity increases the level of consensus in an organization. I would argue that a more diverse team, board, or organization *should* be more effective at combatting consensus. In reality, however, groupthink does not discriminate, but it does feast on sameness.

In their experiment with staunch liberal and staunch conservative groups of Colorado residents, *Wiser* authors Sunstein and Hastie found deliberations increased consensus within groups. The like-minded became more like-minded, and more extreme versions of predeliberation positions resulted.[30] This finding was consistent with many previous social psychology studies.[31] Again, deliberation can reduce the diversity of thought within a group. In many instances, traditional group deliberation is akin to a confirmation exercise rather than constructive discourse.

Another organizational phenomenon colored in sameness is that of *fit*. You may hear the term if discussing the strategic addition of product lines, new business units, or the adoption of new technologies. During due diligence for an acquisition, it's appropriate to ask if a new venture fits with the existing business, current technology platforms, or corporate culture.

The concept of fit is mostly used with regard to personnel. When hiring new employees, assembling a project team, or adding a board member, candidates are evaluated on the basis of being a good fit. Why are we fixated on fit? Are we that insecure? If everyone is such a good fit, are we really that diverse and open to novel ideas? Probably not.

I realize that you want good working relationships among people in a group, and I admit to enjoying group work more when I like the people in my group. But healthy discourse and superior group results can be enhanced by misfits now and again. Maybe we should purposefully try to add people that are not ideal, cookie cutterlike fits. Don't hire people unfit for the task, but hire some misfits. This will encourage diversity of thought, challenge the status quo, add some edge to the risk profile, and likely increase out-of-the-box thinking. Adding misfits should reduce the chance of group consensus.

All for One And...

Recall how mental models are those ready-made, quick decision frameworks that we benefit from so often. Next we'll discuss *shared* mental models among group members in terms of two categories: task-related and team-related. Shared mental models of the task-oriented variety involve operationally relevant aspects such as steps to complete a task and specific knowledge needed to perform individual assignments. Team-related shared mental models are composed of knowing the skills and knowledge of all team members, at least to some generalized extent.[32] For example, a team-related shared mental model would include an understanding of the project's overall schedule, visibility, and level of priority within the organization.

Team members may implicitly hold similar views on team goals and priorities, yet they may explicitly communicate a different sense of goals given team dynamics. They may try to placate other team members due to social or political pressures. Variations in explicit attitudes could weaken a team's ability to reach an explicit consensus.[33]

To mitigate sociopolitical pressures and group biases, it would be wise to have members write down their thoughts and positions prior to speaking about their opinions in a group setting. The team should then read one another's opinions before going to the speaking phase where charisma, power, halo effects, and 800-pound gorillas set the tone. Also, groups should rotate the batting order of who speaks first, as was the past practice of the U.S. Supreme Court, which had the least senior members of the court vote first.[34]

A recently published study in the *Academy of Management Review* argued that in spite of shared consensus on team goals, individuals may act on accomplishing subconscious goals during their individual task time. Researchers attribute this goal switching to a lack of a self-regulating mechanism within the individual. This may be more prevalent with certain individuals over long periods of time while working alone or apart from team-monitored activities.[35] The implication here is that groupthink tendencies may lessen as time and space barriers increase.

As you may have guessed, there is no consensus on consensus. But there have been attempts at categorizing consensus in terms of cognitive and emotional dimensions. For example, a *strong consensus* entails both a common understanding (cognition) and commitment (emotion) to a decision or strategy. An example would be all supervisors knowing that bridge construction needs to be completed by June 1 to ensure that the crew receives a bonus. Knowledge of this incentive creates a shared sense of urgency. A *weak consensus* does not have a shared understanding and it exhibits low commitment among members. *Blind devotion* describes individuals that are highly committed but may not comprehend why. Lastly, *informed skeptics* possess a clear understanding of the issues yet are not committed to the cause. The informed skeptics in this framework could serve as excellent devil's advocates, but their low commitment level may harm the attainment of group goals due to lack of effort, not caring, or poor execution. These skeptics are more valuable during early stages of group work.[36] Perhaps you've witnessed some of your organization's best and brightest not performing up to their potential during team or organizationwide initiatives. It's very likely they do not believe in the direction of the program.

We should note that the research literature draws a distinction between group decision making and interactive decision making. Interactive decision making permits individuals to "consult with others but make their final decisions alone." Individuals can thus selectively "use or ignore the information they collect during social interaction."[37] By extension, one can argue that a strong group leader may use this interactive approach, rightly or wrongly, and proclaim his or her solution under the guise of a group edict.

Incidentally, there is evidence that interactive decision making does indeed increase decision confidence but does not improve decision quality or accuracy.[38] Regarding group decision quality, there has been some interesting research of late funded by MIT's Center for Collective Intelligence. One study found three main characteristics that contributed to making teams smarter (measured by collective intelligence tasks). These characteristics are as follows:

- More balanced contributions from all team members. This alone should help mitigate the incidence of wrongful consensus.
- Smarter teams had members who scored higher on a "Reading the Mind in the Eyes" exercise. This test measures your ability to ascertain emotional states of others by looking only into their eyes.
- Teams with more women scored higher, primarily due to their performance on the "Reading the Mind" portion of the task set.

Additional studies, performed in online environments to mimic the conditions of virtual teams, have produced similar results.[39] We can look forward to more group decision research such as this in the near future.

A Lone Wolf's Wrap-Up on Consensus

In summary, group leaders should avoid setting a biased tone for group decisions. They should keep their position power and opinions in check until group input has been objectively gathered. Groups should encourage and be tolerant of disagreement, diversity of thought, and minority opinions. Note, a group's collective zeal for concurrence and superficial harmony may often trump the motivation for accuracy and truth. Given these dynamics, a healthy mix of anxiety and devil's advocacy should be welcomed to keep the group from getting complacent and being too agreeable.

If consensus had a better track record for arriving at the best possible decision, I would be all for it. But it doesn't. A correct consensus usually involves a more obvious decision. If an obvious solution arises, why bother convening a group or committee in the first place? And if you get the sense that your group thought process is hell bent on consensus, try invoking some wisdom from Warren Buffett, who said, "My idea of a group decision is to look in the mirror."[40]

Contra Maxims for Consensus Decision Making

Good groups foster dissent. A little negativity can be a big plus for group decision making. Beware of the group consensus. Devil's advocates may be our better angels!

Notes

1. Jonathan Rodkin and Francesca Levy, "Focus on MBA," *Bloomberg Businessweek*, 13–19 Apr 2015, 43.

2. Daniel Kahneman, *Thinking, Fast and Slow* (New York, NY: Farrar, Straus and Giroux, 2011).

3. Malcolm Gladwell, *Blink: The Power of Thinking without Thinking* (New York, NY: Little, Brown and Company, 2005), 14.

4. Kahneman, *Thinking, Fast and Slow*

5. Ibid.

6. *Olympia's List*, 2012, http://www.olympiaslist.org/ (accessed Sep 15, 2015).

7. Irving Janis, *Victims of Groupthink: A Psychological Study of Foreign-Policy Decisions and Fiascoes* (Boston, MA: Houghton Mifflin, 1972).

8. Glen Whyte, "Groupthink Reconsidered," *Academy of Management Review* 14, no. 1 (1989): 40–56.

9. Cass Sunstein and Reid Hastie, *Wiser: Getting Beyond Groupthink to Make Groups Smarter* (Boston, MA: Harvard Business Review Press, 2015), 23.

10. Ibid.

11. Ibid., 25–27.

12. Ibid., 53.

13. Ibid., 78.

14. Ibid., 34.

15. Warren Bennis and Patricia Ward Biederman, *Organizing Genius: The Secrets of Creative Collaboration* (New York, NY: Basic, 1997), 209.

16. Paul Rogers and Marcia Blenko, "Who Has the D?" In *On Making Smart Decisions* (Boston, MA: Harvard Business Review Press, 2013), 100.

17. Sunstein and Hastie, *Wiser: Getting Beyond Groupthink,* 11.

18. Adam Bryant, "Designate a Devil's Advocate," *The New York Times,* 9 Aug 2015, BU 2.

19. Kahneman, *Thinking, Fast and Slow,* 264–265.

20. James Surowiecki, *The Wisdom of Crowds* (New York, NY: Anchor Books, 2005), 4.

21. Ibid., xix.

22. Mark Klein, "How to Harvest Collective Wisdom and Complex Problems: An Introduction to the MIT Deliberatorium," MIT Center for Collective Intelligence, 2011, http://cci.mit.edu/klein/deliberatorium.html (accessed Jul 28, 2015).

23. MIT Center for Collective Intelligence, "An Introduction to the MIT Deliberatorium," [Video] http://cci.mit.edu/deliberatoriumresearchpage.html (accessed Jul 28, 2015).

24. Ibid.

25. Klein, "How to Harvest Collective Wisdom"

26. Sydney Finkelstein and Ann Mooney, "Not the Usual Suspects: How to Use Board Process to Make Boards Better," *Academy of Management Executive* 17, no. 2 (2003): 101–113.

27. Donald Hambrick, Vilmos Misangyi and Chuljin Park, "The Quad Model for Identifying a Corporate Director's Potential for Effective Monitoring: Toward a New Theory of Board Sufficiency," *Academy of Management Review* 40, no. 3 (2015): 323–344.

28. Charlan J. Nemeth, "Managing Innovation: When Less is More," *California Management Review* 40, no. 1 (1997): 59–74.

29. William Klepper, *The CEO's Boss: Tough Love in the Boardroom* (New York, NY: Columbia University Press, 2010).

30. Sunstein and Hastie, *Wiser: Getting Beyond Groupthink*, 83.

31. Nemeth, "Managing Innovation"

32. Mark Healey, Timo Vuori and Gerard Hodgkinson, "When Teams Agree While Disagreeing: Reflexion and Reflection in Shared Cognition," *Academy of Management Review* 40, no. 3 (2015): 399–422.

33. Ibid., 408.

34. *The Economist*, "Free Exchange: Meeting Up," 4 Apr 2015, 72.

35. Healey et al., "When Teams Agree While Disagreeing"

36. Stephen Floyd and Bill Wooldridge, "Managing Strategic Consensus: The Foundation of Effective Implementation," *Academy of Management Executive* 6, no. 4 (1992): 27–39.

37. Chip Heath and Rich Gonzalez (1995). "Interaction with Others Increases Decision Confidence but not Decision Quality: Evidence against Information Collection Views of Interactive Decision Making," *Organizational Behavior and Human Decision Processes* 61, no. 3 (1995): 306.

38. Ibid., 305–326.

39. David Engel, Anita Woolley, Lisa Jing, Christopher Chabris and Thomas Malone, "Reading the Mind in the Eyes or Reading Between the Lines? Theory of Mind Predicts Collective Intelligence Equally Well Online and Face-to-Face," *PloS One Journal*, 16 Dec 2014, DOI: 10.1371/journal.pone.0115212

40. Hannah Clark, "Words of Wisdom from Warren Buffett," *Forbes*, 1 Jan 2007, http://www.forbes.com/2007/01/10/leadership-managing-money-lead-manage-cx_hc_0110buffett.html (accessed Jan 4, 2015).

Index

OTHER TITLES IN THE HUMAN RESOURCE MANAGEMENT AND ORGANIZATIONAL BEHAVIOR COLLECTION

- *The Illusion of Inclusion: Global Inclusion, Unconscious Bias, and the Bottom Line* by Helen Turnbull
- *On All Cylinders: The Entrepreneur's Handbook* by Ron Robinson
- *The Resilience Advantage: Stop Managing Stress and Find Your Resilience* by Richard S. Citrin and Alan Weiss
- *Successful Interviewing: A Talent-Focused Approach to Successful Recruitment and Selection* by Tony Miller
- *HR Analytics and Innovations in Workforce Planning* by Tony Miller
- *Success: Theory and Practice* by Michael Edmondson
- *Leading The Positive Organization: Actions, Tools, and Processes* by Thomas N. Duening, Donald G. Gardner, Dustin Bluhm, Andrew J. Czaplewski, and Thomas Martin Key
- *Performance Leadership* by Karen Moustafa Leonard and Fatma Pakdil
- *The New Leader: Harnessing The Power of Creativity to Produce Change* by Renee Kosiarek
- *Employee LEAPS: Leveraging Engagement by Applying Positive Strategies* by Kevin E. Phillips
- *Feet to the Fire: How to Exemplify and Create the Accountability That Creates Great Companies* by Lorraine A. Moore

Announcing the Business Expert Press Digital Library

Concise e-books business students need for classroom and research

This book can also be purchased in an e-book collection by your library as

- *a one-time purchase,*
- *that is owned forever,*
- *allows for simultaneous readers,*
- *has no restrictions on printing, and*
- *can be downloaded as PDFs from within the library community.*

Our digital library collections are a great solution to beat the rising cost of textbooks. E-books can be loaded into their course management systems or onto students' e-book readers.
The **Business Expert Press** digital libraries are very affordable, with no obligation to buy in future years. For more information, please visit **www.businessexpertpress.com/librarians**.
To set up a trial in the United States, please email **sales@businessexpertpress.com**.

www.ingramcontent.com/pod-product-compliance
Lightning Source LLC
Chambersburg PA
CBHW062042200326
41519CB00017B/5103